ITALIAN
at home

Publications International, Ltd.

Front cover photography and photography on pages 4 (top right), 6, 8, 10, 12, 14, 16, 18, 20, 22, 23, 24, 26 and 160 (top right) by Shutterstock.

Pictured on the back cover *(clockwise from top left):* Prosciutto-Wrapper Snapper *(page 136),* Espresso Chocolate Cheesecake *(page 180)* and Classic Fettuccine Alfredo *(page 38).*

ISBN-13: 978-1-60553-171-7
ISBN-10: 1-60553-171-5

Library of Congress Control Number: 2009939444

Manufactured in China.

8 7 6 5 4 3 2 1

Microwave Cooking: Microwave ovens vary in wattage. Use the cooking times as guidelines and check for doneness before adding more time.

Preparation/Cooking Times: Preparation times are based on the approximate amount of time required to assemble the recipe before cooking, baking, chilling or serving. These times include preparation steps such as measuring, chopping and mixing. The fact that some preparations and cooking can be done simultaneously is taken into account. Preparation of optional ingredients and serving suggestions is not included.

Publications International, Ltd.

Table of Contents

MENU

Calamari Salad

Marinated Antipasto

Caprese-Style Tartlettes

Fried Calamari with
Tartar Sauce

Oysters Romano

Arancini

Caponata

Asparagus & Prosciutto
Antipasto

Margherita Panini Bites

Asiago Toasts

Clams Posilippo

Eggplant Rolls

Caramelized Onion Focaccia

Starters & Small Plates

Calamari Salad

¼ cup plus 1 tablespoon extra-virgin olive oil, divided
1½ pounds cleaned squid (body tubes only)
   Juice of 1 lemon
 1 can (about 15 ounces) cannellini beans, rinsed and drained
 1 cup thinly sliced celery
 1 cup thinly sliced red bell pepper
½ cup thinly sliced white onion
 3 tablespoons red wine vinegar
 2 tablespoons chopped fresh Italian parsley
 1 tablespoon chopped fresh basil
 1 tablespoon chopped fresh oregano
 2 cloves garlic, minced
 1 teaspoon salt
½ teaspoon red pepper flakes

1. Heat 1 tablespoon oil in large nonstick skillet over medium-high heat. Add squid; cook 2 minutes per side. Let cool slightly; cut into rings. Place in large bowl; drizzle with lemon juice. Add beans, celery, bell pepper and onion.

2. Whisk vinegar, parsley, basil, oregano, garlic, salt and red pepper flakes in small bowl. Slowly whisk in remaining ¼ cup oil until blended. Pour over squid mixture and toss gently. Refrigerate at least 1 hour. Serve chilled or at room temperature.   *Makes 6 servings*

Marinated Antipasto

¼ cup extra-virgin olive oil

2 tablespoons balsamic vinegar

1 clove garlic, minced

½ teaspoon sugar

½ teaspoon salt

¼ teaspoon black pepper

1 pint (2 cups) cherry tomatoes

1 can (14 ounces) quartered artichoke hearts, drained

8 ounces small balls or cubes fresh mozzarella cheese

1 cup drained pitted kalamata olives

¼ cup sliced fresh basil leaves

    Lettuce leaves

1. Whisk oil, vinegar, garlic, sugar, salt and pepper in medium bowl. Add tomatoes, artichokes, mozzarella cheese, olives and basil; toss to coat. Let stand at room temperature 30 minutes.

2. Line platter with lettuce. Arrange tomato mixture over lettuce; serve at room temperature.   *Makes about 5 cups*

Caprese-Style Tartlettes

3 tomatoes
3 tablespoons pesto
1 sheet frozen puff pastry, thawed
6 ounces fresh mozzarella cheese
2 tablespoons kalamata olive tapenade

1. Slice each tomato into 4 slices (about ⅓ inch thick). Discard tops and bottoms. Place in resealable food storage bag with pesto, tossing to coat. Refrigerate 30 minutes or overnight.

2. Preheat oven to 425°F. Line baking sheet with parchment paper.

3. Cut out 6 (4-inch) rounds from sheet of pastry. Place rounds on prepared baking sheet. Top each round with 2 slices marinated tomato. Bake 12 minutes or until pastry is golden brown and puffed.

4. Preheat broiler. Slice mozzarella cheese into 6 (¼-inch-thick) slices. Top each tart with 1 slice cheese. Broil 1 minute or until cheese is melted. Top tarts evenly with tapenade. Serve warm. *Makes 6 tartlettes*

Tip

Tapenade is a Provençal condiment made from minced olives, anchovies, capers, olive oil and seasonings. It is sold in large supermarkets and specialty food stores.

Fried Calamari with Tartar Sauce

Tartar Sauce (page 14)
1 pound cleaned squid (body tubes, tentacles or a combination), rinsed and patted dry
¾ cup plain dry bread crumbs
1 egg
1 tablespoon milk
Vegetable oil
Lemon wedges (optional)

1. Prepare Tartar Sauce; set aside. Line baking sheet with waxed paper. Cut squid into ¼-inch rings.

2. Spread bread crumbs on plate. Beat egg and milk in small bowl. Add squid; stir to coat well. Transfer squid to bread crumbs; toss to coat. Place on prepared baking sheet. Refrigerate 15 minutes.

3. Heat 1½ inches oil in large heavy saucepan to 350°F; adjust heat to maintain temperature of oil.* Fry squid in batches, 8 to 10 pieces at a time, 45 seconds or until golden brown. (Squid will pop and spatter during frying; do not stand too close to saucepan.) *Do not overcook squid or it will become tough.* Remove with slotted spoon; drain on paper towels.

4. Serve immediately with Tartar Sauce and lemon wedges, if desired.

Makes 2 to 3 servings

*To shallow fry squid, heat about ¼ inch oil in large skillet over medium-high heat; reduce heat to medium. Add single layer of squid to oil without crowding. Cook 1 minute per side or until golden brown. Drain on paper towels.

continued on page 14

Starters & Small Plates

Fried Calamari with Tartar Sauce, continued

Tartar Sauce

1⅓ cups mayonnaise
2 tablespoons chopped fresh Italian parsley
1 green onion, thinly sliced
1 tablespoon drained capers, minced
1 small sweet gherkin or pickle, minced

Combine all ingredients in small bowl; mix well. Cover; refrigerate until ready to serve.   *Makes about 1⅓ cups*

Oysters Romano

12 oysters, shucked and on the half shell
2 slices bacon, cut into 12 pieces
½ cup Italian seasoned dry bread crumbs
2 tablespoons butter, melted
½ teaspoon garlic salt
6 tablespoons grated Romano or Parmesan cheese
Fresh chives (optional)

1. Preheat oven to 375°F. Place shells with oysters on baking sheet. Top each oyster with 1 piece bacon. Bake 10 minutes or until bacon is crisp.

2. Combine bread crumbs, butter and garlic salt in small bowl. Spoon mixture over oysters; sprinkle with Romano cheese. Bake 5 minutes or until cheese melts. Garnish with chives.   *Makes 12 oysters*

Arancini

Risotto alla Milanese (page 45)
1½ cups Italian seasoned dry bread crumbs
  3 egg whites
 12 (½-inch) pieces fresh mozzarella cheese
 12 (½-inch) pieces Parmigiano-Reggiano cheese
 12 (¼-inch) cubes ham
  2 cups canola oil

1. Prepare Risotto alla Milanese. Spread on nonstick baking sheet; cool completely. Spread bread crumbs on plate. Beat egg whites in small bowl.

2. Line baking sheet with waxed paper. Working with 2 tablespoons risotto at a time, flatten into 3-inch disc. Place 1 piece each of mozzarella cheese, Parmigiano-Reggiano cheese and ham in center of disc. Fold edges up to cover filling, gently pinching seams to seal. Roll between palms to form ball roughly the size of a large egg.

3. Dip ball in bread crumbs, then egg whites, then again in bread crumbs. Place on prepared baking sheet. Repeat until all risotto is used. Cover; refrigerate 1 hour or overnight.

4. Heat oil in large deep skillet to 360°F. Cook 1 minute per side or until golden brown. Transfer to wire rack. Serve warm.

Makes 12 servings

Caponata

1 medium eggplant (about 1 pound), peeled and cut into
 ½-inch pieces

1 can (about 14 ounces) diced tomatoes

1 onion, chopped

1 red bell pepper, cut into ½-inch pieces

½ cup salsa

¼ cup olive oil

2 tablespoons capers, drained

2 tablespoons balsamic vinegar

3 cloves garlic, minced

1 teaspoon dried oregano

¼ teaspoon salt

⅓ cup packed fresh basil leaves, cut into thin strips
 Toasted Italian or French bread slices

Slow Cooker Directions

1. Combine eggplant, tomatoes, onion, bell pepper, salsa, oil, capers, vinegar, garlic, oregano and salt in slow cooker. Cover; cook on LOW 7 to 8 hours or until vegetables are crisp-tender.

2. Stir in basil. Serve at room temperature with toasted bread.

Makes about 5¼ cups

Asparagus & Prosciutto Antipasto

12 asparagus spears (about 8 ounces)
2 ounces cream cheese, softened
¼ cup (1 ounce) crumbled Gorgonzola cheese
¼ teaspoon black pepper
1 package (3 to 4 ounces) thinly sliced prosciutto

1. Trim and discard tough ends of asparagus spears. Simmer asparagus in salted water in large skillet 4 to 5 minutes or until crisp-tender. Drain; rinse with cold water until cool. Drain; pat dry with paper towels.

2. Combine cream cheese, Gorgonzola cheese and pepper in small bowl; mix well. Cut prosciutto slices in half crosswise to make 12 pieces. Spread cream cheese mixture evenly over 1 side of each prosciutto slice.

3. Wrap each asparagus spear with prosciutto slice. Serve at room temperature or slightly chilled.   *Makes 12 appetizers*

Tip

Prosciutto, the Italian word for ham, is seasoned, cured and air-dried, not smoked. It is usually sold in very thin slices. Look for the imported Parma or less expensive domestic substitutes in delis and Italian food markets.

Margherita Panini Bites

1 loaf (16 ounces) ciabatta or crusty Italian bread, cut into
    16 (½-inch) slices

8 teaspoons pesto

16 fresh basil leaves

8 slices fresh mozzarella cheese

24 thin slices plum tomato (about 3 tomatoes)

   Olive oil

Heat grill pan over medium-high heat. Spread 1 side of 8 slices bread evenly with pesto. Top with basil, mozzarella cheese, tomato and remaining bread. Brush both sides of sandwiches with oil. Grill 5 minutes or until lightly browned and cheese is melted. Cut each sandwich into 4 pieces. Serve warm.   *Makes 32 panini bites*

Asiago Toasts

⅓ cup HELLMANN'S® or BEST FOODS® Mayonnaise Dressing with
    Extra Virgin Olive Oil

1 cup shredded Asiago or Parmesan-Reggiano cheese

1 clove garlic, finely chopped

1 tablespoon chopped fresh oregano leaves *or* 1 teaspoon dried
    oregano leaves, crushed (optional)

1 tablespoon chopped flat-leaf parsley (optional)

½ French baguette, cut into 18 slices

1. In small bowl, combine all ingredients except baguette.

2. On baking sheet, arrange baguette slices in a single layer; spread cheese mixture. Broil until cheese is melted and golden, about 3 minutes.

Makes 18 appetizers

Clams Posilippo

2 dozen cherrystone clams, well scrubbed
½ cup finely chopped red or yellow bell pepper
½ cup finely chopped plum tomatoes
½ cup finely chopped green onions
¼ cup chopped Canadian bacon or boiled ham
¼ cup *Frank's® RedHot®* Original Cayenne Pepper Sauce
2 tablespoons olive oil
2 tablespoons grated Parmesan cheese

1. Place clams in large nonstick skillet; add ¼ cup water. Cook, covered, over medium heat 6 to 8 minutes or until clams begin to open, removing them to dish as they open. Rinse clams under water to remove excess sand, if necessary. Remove top shells; discard. With paring knife, loosen clam meat from bottom shell. Place clams in shallow ovenproof baking dish.

2. Preheat oven to 400°F. Combine bell pepper, tomatoes, onions, bacon, *Frank's RedHot* Sauce and oil in small bowl. Spoon about 1 tablespoon mixture over each clam. Sprinkle with cheese.

3. Bake clams 10 minutes or until heated through.   *Makes 6 servings*

Tip

When buying clams in the shell, be sure shells are tightly closed. If the shell is slightly open, tap it lightly. It should immediately snap shut. If it doesn't, then the clam is dead and should be discarded.

Eggplant Rolls

1 large eggplant (about 1¼ pounds)
3 tablespoons extra-virgin olive oil
   Salt and black pepper
1 cup whole milk ricotta cheese
½ cup grated Asiago cheese
¼ cup julienned or chopped sun-dried tomatoes, packed in oil
¼ cup chopped fresh basil or Italian parsley
⅛ teaspoon red pepper flakes
   Cherry tomatoes, halved (optional)
   Fresh thyme (optional)

1. Preheat broiler. Trim stem end from eggplant; discard. Peel eggplant, if desired. Cut eggplant lengthwise into 6 slices about ¼ inch thick. Brush both sides of eggplant slices with oil; sprinkle with salt and pepper. Place on rack of broiler pan.

2. Broil 4 inches from heat 4 to 5 minutes per side or until golden brown and slightly softened. Let cool to room temperature.

3. Combine ricotta cheese, Asiago cheese, sun-dried tomatoes, basil and red pepper flakes in small bowl; mix well. Spread mixture evenly over eggplant slices. Roll up and cut each roll in half crosswise. Arrange, seam side down, on serving platter. Garnish with cherry tomatoes and thyme. Serve warm or at room temperature.   *Makes 6 servings*

Caramelized Onion Focaccia

2 tablespoons plus 1 teaspoon olive oil, divided
4 onions, cut in half and thinly sliced
½ teaspoon salt
2 tablespoons water
1 tablespoon chopped fresh rosemary leaves
¼ teaspoon black pepper
1 loaf (1 pound) frozen bread dough, thawed
1 cup (4 ounces) shredded fontina cheese
¼ cup grated Parmesan cheese

1. Heat 2 tablespoons oil in large skillet over medium-high heat. Add onions and salt; cook 10 minutes or until onions begin to brown, stirring occasionally. Stir in water. Reduce heat to medium; partially cover and cook 20 minutes or until onions are deep golden brown, stirring occasionally. Remove from heat; stir in rosemary and pepper. Set aside.

2. Brush 13×9-inch baking pan with remaining 1 teaspoon oil. Roll out dough into 13×9-inch rectangle on lightly floured surface. Transfer to prepared pan; cover and let rise in warm, draft-free place 30 minutes.

3. Preheat oven to 375°F. Prick dough all over (about 12 times) with fork. Sprinkle fontina cheese over dough; top with caramelized onions. Sprinkle with Parmesan cheese.

4. Bake 18 to 20 minutes or until golden brown. Remove from pan to wire rack. Cut into pieces; serve warm. *Makes 12 servings*

Menu

Spaghetti & Meatballs

Chicken Piccata

Baked Ziti

Eggplant Parmigiana

Classic Fettuccine Alfredo

Shrimp Scampi

Garlic Spinach Lasagna

Veal Parmesan

Risotto alla Milanese

Pasta with Creamy Vodka Sauce

Milanese Pork Chops

Potato Gnocchi with Tomato Sauce

Five Mushroom Risotto

Quick Pasta Puttanesca

Chicken Marsala with Fettuccine

Italian Sausage and Peppers

Chicken Saltimbocca

Essential
Italian Dishes

Essential Italian Dishes

Spaghetti & Meatballs

Nonstick cooking spray
6 ounces uncooked spaghetti
¾ pound ground beef
¼ pound hot turkey Italian sausage, casing removed
1 egg white
2 tablespoons plain dry bread crumbs
1 teaspoon dried oregano
2 cups marinara sauce
2 tablespoons grated Parmesan cheese
3 tablespoons chopped fresh basil

1. Preheat oven to 450°F. Coat baking sheet with cooking spray. Cook spaghetti according to package directions. Drain; cover and keep warm.

2. Combine beef, sausage, egg white, bread crumbs and oregano in medium bowl; mix well. Shape mixture into 16 (1½-inch) meatballs. Place on prepared baking sheet; coat with cooking spray. Bake 12 minutes, turning once.

3. Pour marinara sauce into large skillet; add meatballs. Cook and stir over medium heat 9 minutes or until sauce is heated through and meatballs are cooked through (160°F). Serve spaghetti with meatballs and sauce; sprinkle with Parmesan cheese and basil.

Makes 4 servings

Chicken Piccata

  3 tablespoons all-purpose flour
½ teaspoon salt
¼ teaspoon black pepper
  4 boneless skinless chicken breasts
  2 teaspoons olive oil
  1 teaspoon butter
  2 cloves garlic, minced
¾ cup chicken broth
  1 tablespoon fresh lemon juice
  2 tablespoons chopped fresh Italian parsley
  1 tablespoon capers, drained

1. Combine flour, salt and pepper in shallow dish. Reserve 1 tablespoon flour mixture.

2. Pound chicken between waxed paper to ½-inch thickness. Coat chicken with remaining flour mixture, shaking off excess.

3. Heat oil and butter in large nonstick skillet over medium heat. Add chicken; cook 4 to 5 minutes per side or until no longer pink in center. Transfer to serving platter; cover loosely with foil.

4. Add garlic to same skillet; cook and stir 1 minute. Add reserved flour mixture; cook and stir 1 minute. Add broth and lemon juice; cook 2 minutes or until thickened, stirring frequently. Stir in parsley and capers; spoon sauce over chicken.   *Makes 4 servings*

Baked Ziti

REYNOLDS WRAP® Non-Stick Foil
1 pound ground beef, browned and drained
4 cups (32-ounce jar) chunky garden-style pasta sauce
1 tablespoon Italian seasoning, divided
1 package (16 ounces) ziti pasta, cooked and drained
1 package (8 ounces) shredded mozzarella cheese, divided
1 container (16 ounces) ricotta cheese or cottage cheese
1 egg
¼ cup grated Parmesan cheese, divided

Preheat oven to 350°F.

Combine ground beef, pasta sauce and 2 teaspoons Italian seasoning. Stir pasta into meat sauce; spread half of mixture evenly in pan. Top with half of mozzarella cheese.

Combine ricotta cheese, egg, 2 tablespoons Parmesan cheese and remaining Italian seasoning; spread over mozzarella cheese in pan. Spread remaining pasta mixture over ricotta cheese mixture. Sprinkle with remaining mozzarella and Parmesan cheeses.

Cover with Reynolds Wrap Non-Stick Foil with non-stick (dull) side toward food.

Bake 45 minutes. Remove foil cover and continue baking 15 minutes or until cheese is melted and lightly browned. Let stand 15 minutes before serving.   *Makes 8 servings*

Prep Time: 20 minutes
Cook Time: 1 hour

Essential Italian Dishes

Eggplant Parmigiana

2 eggs, beaten

¼ cup milk

Dash garlic powder

Dash onion powder

Dash salt

Dash black pepper

½ cup seasoned dry bread crumbs

1 large eggplant (about 1¼ pounds), cut into ½-inch-thick slices

Vegetable oil

1 jar (about 26 ounces) pasta sauce

4 cups (16 ounces) shredded mozzarella cheese

2½ cups (10 ounces) shredded Swiss cheese

¼ cup grated Parmesan cheese

¼ cup grated Romano cheese

1. Preheat oven to 350°F. Combine eggs, milk, garlic powder, onion powder, salt and pepper in shallow dish. Place bread crumbs in another shallow dish. Dip eggplant into egg mixture; coat with bread crumbs.

2. Heat ¼ inch oil in large skillet over medium-high heat. Brown eggplant on both sides in batches; drain on paper towels.

3. Spread 3 tablespoons pasta sauce in bottom of 13×9-inch baking dish. Layer half of eggplant, half of mozzarella cheese, half of Swiss cheese and half of remaining sauce in dish. Repeat layers. Sprinkle with Parmesan and Romano cheeses.

4. Bake 30 minutes or until heated through and cheeses are melted.

Makes 4 servings

Classic Fettuccine Alfredo

12 ounces uncooked fettuccine

⅔ cup whipping cream

6 tablespoons unsalted butter

½ teaspoon salt

Generous dash white pepper

Generous dash ground nutmeg

1 cup grated Parmesan cheese

2 tablespoons chopped fresh Italian parsley

1. Cook pasta according to package directions. Drain well; cover and keep warm in saucepan.

2. Meanwhile, heat cream and butter in large heavy skillet over medium-low heat until butter melts and mixture bubbles, stirring frequently. Cook and stir 2 minutes. Stir in salt, white pepper and nutmeg. Remove from heat. Gradually stir in Parmesan cheese until well blended and smooth. Return to heat until cheese is melted, if necessary. (Do not let sauce bubble or cheese will become lumpy and tough.)

3. Pour sauce over pasta. Cook and stir over low heat 2 to 3 minutes or until sauce thickens and pasta is evenly coated. Sprinkle with parsley. Serve immediately. *Makes 4 servings*

Essential Italian Dishes

Shrimp Scampi

⅓ cup clarified butter (see Tip)
2 to 4 tablespoons minced garlic
1½ pounds large raw shrimp, peeled and deveined
6 green onions, thinly sliced
¼ cup dry white wine
2 tablespoons lemon juice
Chopped fresh Italian parsley
Salt and black pepper
Lemon wedges (optional)

1. Heat clarified butter in large skillet over medium heat. Add garlic; cook and stir 1 to 2 minutes or until softened but not brown. Add shrimp, green onions, wine and lemon juice; cook 2 to 4 minutes or until shrimp are pink and opaque, stirring occasionally.

2. Add parsley; season with salt and pepper. Serve with lemon wedges, if desired.   *Makes 4 to 6 servings*

Tip

To clarify butter, melt butter in small saucepan over low heat. Skim off the white foam that forms on top, then strain the clear butter through cheesecloth. Discard cheesecloth and the milky residue at the bottom of the pan. Clarified butter will keep, covered, in the refrigerator for up to 2 months.

Shrimp Scampi

Essential Italian Dishes

Garlic Spinach Lasagna

12 uncooked lasagna noodles
2 tablespoons olive oil
4 cloves garlic, chopped
2 cups frozen chopped spinach, thawed and squeezed dry
   Salt and black pepper
3 cups ricotta cheese
¾ cup plus 2 tablespoons grated Parmesan cheese, divided
2 eggs, lightly beaten
1 jar (about 24 ounces) pasta sauce
2 cups (8 ounces) shredded provolone or mozzarella cheese

1. Cook lasagna noodles according to package directions. Drain; cover and keep warm. Preheat oven to 350°F.

2. Heat oil in medium nonstick skillet over medium heat. Add garlic; cook 30 seconds. Add spinach; cook and stir 3 minutes. Season with salt and pepper.

3. Combine ricotta cheese, ¾ cup Parmesan cheese and eggs in medium bowl; mix well.

4. Spread a few spoonfuls of pasta sauce in bottom of 13×9-inch baking dish. Layer 4 noodles, 1 cup sauce, half of ricotta mixture, half of spinach mixture and ½ cup provolone cheese in dish. Repeat layers. Top with remaining noodles, sauce, 1 cup provolone cheese and 2 tablespoons Parmesan cheese.

5. Cover tightly with foil. Bake 30 minutes or until hot and bubbly. Remove foil; bake 15 minutes or until browned.   *Makes 8 servings*

Essential Italian Dishes

Veal Parmesan

½ cup CONTADINA® Italian Bread Crumbs

¼ cup (1 ounce) grated Parmesan cheese

1 pound thin veal cutlets

1 egg, lightly beaten

3 tablespoons olive oil, divided

4 ounces mozzarella cheese, thinly sliced

¼ cup finely chopped onion

1 clove garlic, minced

1 can (8 ounces) CONTADINA Tomato Sauce

1 tablespoon chopped fresh oregano *or* 1 teaspoon dried oregano leaves, crushed

Additional grated Parmesan cheese (optional)

1. Combine bread crumbs and ¼ cup Parmesan cheese in shallow dish. Dip veal into egg; coat with crumb mixture.

2. Heat 2 tablespoons oil in large skillet over medium-high heat. Add veal; cook until golden brown on both sides. Drain on paper towels. Place veal on ovenproof platter; top with mozzarella cheese.

3. Bake in preheated 350°F oven for 5 to 10 minutes or until cheese is melted.

4. Meanwhile, heat remaining oil in medium saucepan. Add onion and garlic; sauté until tender.

5. Stir in tomato sauce and oregano. Bring to a boil. Reduce heat to low; simmer, uncovered, for 5 to 10 minutes or until heated through. Serve sauce over veal. Sprinkle with additional Parmesan cheese, if desired.

Makes 4 servings

Risotto alla Milanese

4 cups chicken or vegetable broth
2 tablespoons butter
2 tablespoons olive oil
1 shallot, minced
1 cup Arborio rice
¼ cup white wine
1 generous pinch saffron threads, ground to a powder
¼ cup grated Parmesan cheese
Salt and black pepper

1. Bring broth to a boil in medium saucepan over medium-high heat. Reduce heat to low; keep warm.

2. Heat butter and oil in deep saucepan over medium-high heat. Add shallot; cook and stir 30 seconds or just until beginning to brown.

3. Add rice; cook and stir 1 to 2 minutes or until edges of rice become translucent. Add wine and saffron; cook and stir until wine evaporates.

4. Reduce heat to medium-low. Add ½ cup broth, stirring constantly until broth is absorbed. Repeat until all broth is used. Stir in Parmesan cheese. Season with salt and pepper.

Makes 4 servings

Essential Italian Dishes

Pasta with Creamy Vodka Sauce

6 ounces uncooked campanelle or bowtie pasta
1 tablespoon unsalted butter
3 plum tomatoes, seeded and chopped
2 cloves garlic, minced
3 tablespoons vodka
½ cup whipping cream
¼ teaspoon salt
¼ teaspoon red pepper flakes
⅓ cup grated Parmesan cheese
2 tablespoons snipped fresh chives

1. Cook pasta according to package directions. Drain; cover and keep warm in saucepan.

2. Melt butter in large skillet over medium heat. Add tomatoes and garlic; cook 3 minutes, stirring frequently. Add vodka; simmer 2 minutes or until most of liquid has evaporated.

3. Stir in cream, salt and red pepper flakes. Simmer 2 to 3 minutes or until slightly thickened. Remove from heat; let stand 2 minutes. Stir in Parmesan cheese until melted.

4. Add sauce and chives to pasta; toss until pasta is coated. Serve immediately. *Makes 4 servings*

Essential Italian Dishes

Milanese Pork Chops

2 tablespoons all-purpose flour
½ teaspoon salt
½ teaspoon black pepper
1 egg
1 teaspoon water
¼ cup seasoned dry bread crumbs
¼ cup grated Parmesan cheese
4 boneless pork loin chops, cut ¾ inch thick
1 tablespoon olive oil
1 tablespoon butter
Lemon wedges

1. Preheat oven to 400°F. Combine flour, salt and pepper in shallow dish. Beat egg and water in shallow bowl. Combine bread crumbs and Parmesan cheese in separate shallow dish.

2. Dip each pork chop to coat both sides evenly, first in flour mixture, then egg mixture, then in bread crumb mixture. Press coating onto pork. Place on waxed paper; refrigerate 15 minutes. (Chops may be breaded and refrigerated up to 1 hour before cooking.)

3. Heat oil and butter in large ovenproof skillet over medium-high heat until bubbly. Add chops; cook 4 minutes or until golden brown. Turn; transfer skillet to oven. Bake 6 to 8 minutes or until chops are cooked through (160°F). Serve with lemon wedges.   *Makes 4 servings*

Potato Gnocchi with Tomato Sauce

2 pounds baking potatoes (3 or 4 large)
2/3 to 1 cup all-purpose flour, divided
1 egg yolk
1/2 teaspoon salt
1/8 teaspoon ground nutmeg (optional)
1 jar (about 24 ounces) marinara sauce, heated
Chopped fresh basil (optional)

1. Preheat oven to 425°F. Pierce potatoes several times with fork. Bake 1 hour or until soft.

2. Cut potatoes in half lengthwise; cool slightly. Scoop pulp from skins into medium bowl; discard skins. Mash potatoes until smooth. Add 1/3 cup flour, egg yolk, salt and nutmeg, if desired; mix well to form dough.

3. Turn out dough onto well-floured surface. Knead in enough remaining flour to form smooth dough that is not sticky. Divide dough into 4 equal portions. Roll each portion with hands on lightly floured surface into 3/4- to 1-inch-wide rope. Cut each rope into 1-inch pieces; gently press thumb into center of each piece to make indentation. Space gnocchi slightly apart on lightly floured kitchen towel to prevent them from sticking together.

4. Bring 4 quarts salted water to a gentle boil in Dutch oven over high heat. To test gnocchi cooking time, drop several into water; cook 1 minute or until they float to surface. Remove from water with slotted spoon and taste for doneness. Cook remaining gnocchi in batches, removing with slotted spoon to warm serving dish.

5. Top with marinara sauce and serve immediately. Sprinkle with basil, if desired. *Makes 4 servings*

Five Mushroom Risotto

    4 cups chicken or vegetable broth
    4 tablespoons olive oil, divided
    2 tablespoons butter
    1 shallot, minced
    ¼ cup minced fresh Italian parsley
    ¼ cup white wine
    ½ cup *each* shiitake, chanterelle, portobello, oyster and button
        mushrooms, wiped clean and chopped into ½-inch pieces
    ½ teaspoon coarse salt
    1 cup Arborio rice
    ½ cup whipping cream
    ¼ cup grated Parmesan cheese
        Salt and black pepper

1. Bring broth to a boil in medium saucepan over medium-high heat.
Reduce heat to low; keep warm.

2. Heat 2 tablespoons oil and butter in deep saucepan over medium-
high heat. Add shallot; cook and stir 30 seconds or just until beginning
to brown. Add parsley; cook and stir 30 seconds. Add wine; cook and
stir until wine evaporates. Add mushrooms and coarse salt; cook and
stir until mushrooms have softened and reduced their volume by half.
Transfer to medium bowl; set aside.

3. Heat remaining 2 tablespoons oil in same saucepan. Add rice; cook
and stir 1 to 2 minutes or until edges of rice become translucent. Reduce
heat to medium-low. Add ½ cup broth, stirring constantly until broth
is absorbed. Repeat until only ½ cup broth remains. Stir mushroom
mixture into rice. Add remaining broth; cook and stir until absorbed.

4. Remove from heat; add cream and Parmesan cheese, stirring until
cheese is melted. Season with salt and pepper.   *Makes 4 servings*

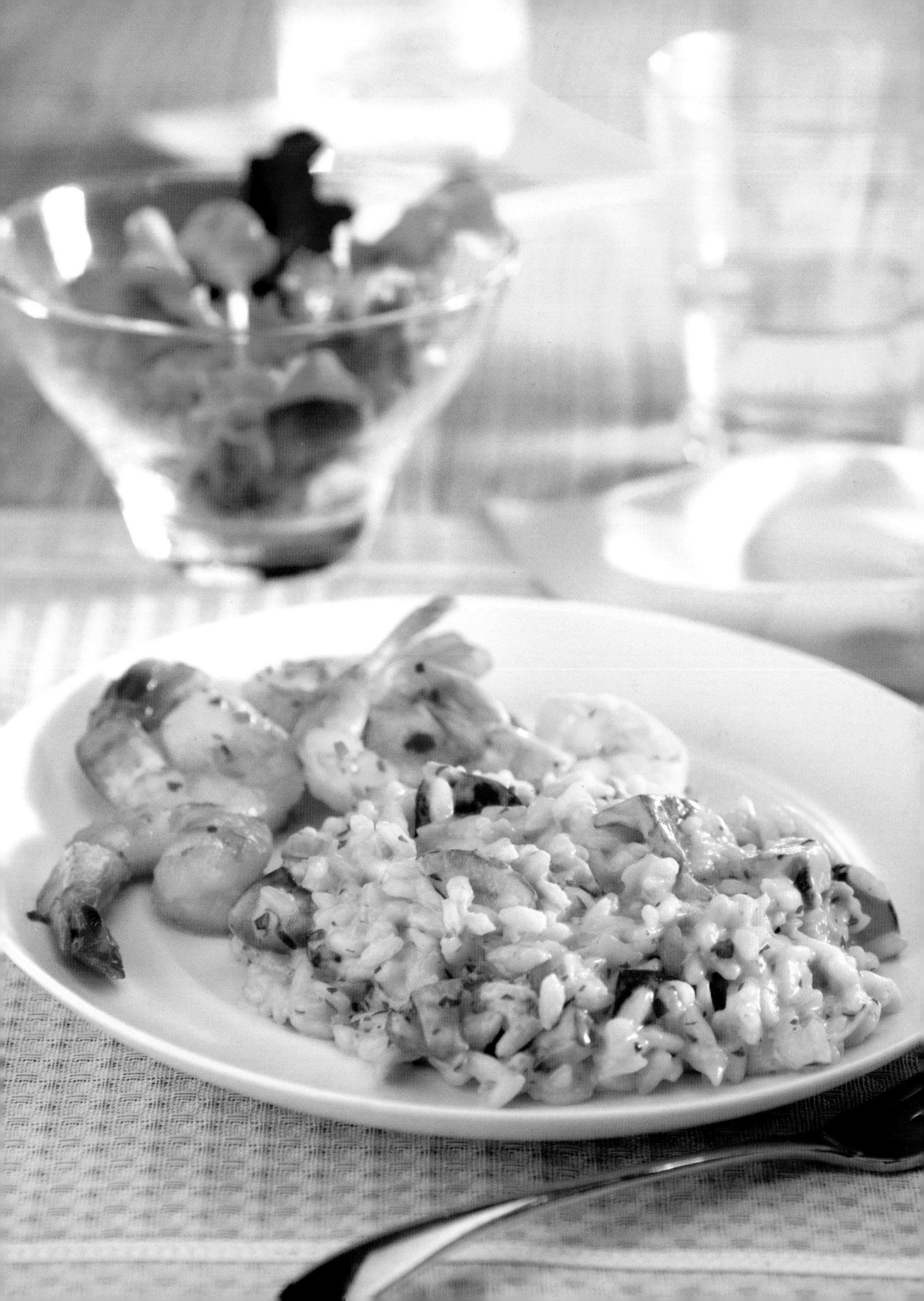

Quick Pasta Puttanesca

1 package (16 ounces) uncooked spaghetti or linguine

3 tablespoons plus 1 teaspoon olive oil, divided

¼ to 1 teaspoon red pepper flakes*

1 tablespoon dried minced onion

1 teaspoon minced garlic

2 cans (6 ounces each) chunk light tuna packed in water, drained

1 can (28 ounces) diced tomatoes

1 can (8 ounces) tomato sauce

24 pitted kalamata or black olives

2 tablespoons capers, drained

*For a mildly spicy dish, use ¼ teaspoon red pepper flakes. For a very spicy dish, use 1 teaspoon red pepper flakes.

1. Cook spaghetti according to package directions; drain and return to saucepan. Add 1 teaspoon oil; toss to coat. Cover and keep warm.

2. Heat remaining 3 tablespoons oil in large skillet over medium-high heat. Add red pepper flakes; cook and stir until sizzling. Add onion and garlic; cook and stir 1 minute. Add tuna; cook and stir 2 to 3 minutes. Add tomatoes, tomato sauce, olives and capers. Cook, stirring frequently, until sauce is heated through.

3. Add sauce to pasta; mix well. Serve immediately.

Makes 6 to 8 servings

Chicken Marsala with Fettuccine

4 boneless skinless chicken breasts
   Salt and black pepper
1 tablespoon vegetable oil
1 onion, chopped
½ cup marsala wine
 2 packages (6 ounces each) sliced cremini mushrooms
½ cup chicken broth
 2 teaspoons Worcestershire sauce
½ cup whipping cream
 2 tablespoons cornstarch
 8 ounces uncooked fettuccine
 2 tablespoons chopped fresh Italian parsley

Slow Cooker Directions

1. Coat slow cooker with nonstick cooking spray. Season chicken with salt and pepper. Transfer to slow cooker.

2. Heat oil in large skillet over medium heat. Add onion; cook and stir until translucent. Add marsala; cook 2 to 3 minutes or until slightly thickened. Stir in mushrooms, broth and Worcestershire sauce. Pour over chicken. Cover; cook on HIGH 1½ to 1¾ hours.

3. Transfer chicken to cutting board; cover and let stand. Blend cream and cornstarch in small bowl until smooth; stir into cooking liquid. Cover; cook 15 minutes or until thickened. Season with salt and pepper.

4. Meanwhile, cook pasta according to package directions. Drain and transfer to large serving bowl. Slice chicken breasts and place on pasta. Top with sauce; sprinkle with parsley. *Makes 6 servings*

Essential Italian Dishes

Italian Sausage and Peppers

3 cups diced red, green and yellow bell peppers
1 onion, cut into thin wedges
3 cloves garlic, minced
4 links hot or mild Italian sausage (about 1 pound)
1 cup pasta or marinara sauce
¼ cup red wine
1 tablespoon cornstarch
1 tablespoon water
   Hot cooked spaghetti (optional)
¼ cup shredded Parmesan or Romano cheese

Slow Cooker Directions

1. Coat slow cooker with cooking spray. Place bell peppers, onion and garlic in slow cooker. Arrange sausage over vegetables. Combine pasta sauce and wine in small bowl; pour over sausage. Cover; cook on LOW 8 to 9 hours or on HIGH 4 to 5 hours.

2. Transfer sausage to serving platter. Cover with foil; keep warm. Let liquid in slow cooker stand 5 minutes. Skim off fat.

3. Turn heat to HIGH. Mix cornstarch with water in small bowl until smooth; add to slow cooker. Cook 15 minutes or until sauce is thickened, stirring once. Serve sauce over sausage and spaghetti, if desired; top with Parmesan cheese.   *Makes 4 servings*

Essential Italian Dishes

Chicken Saltimbocca

¼ cup coarsely chopped fresh basil

2 tablespoons minced fresh chives

2 teaspoons extra-virgin olive oil

1 clove garlic, minced

½ teaspoon *each* dried oregano and dried sage

4 boneless skinless chicken breasts

2 slices (1 ounce each) smoked ham, cut in half

Nonstick cooking spray

½ cup chicken broth

1 cup pasta sauce

2 cups hot cooked spaghetti squash (see Note)

1. Combine basil, chives, oil, garlic, oregano and sage in small bowl. Pound chicken between waxed paper to ½-inch thickness. Spread herb mixture evenly over chicken; top with ham. Roll up; secure with toothpicks.

2. Spray medium skillet with cooking spray; heat over medium-high heat. Cook chicken, seam side up, 2 to 3 minutes or until browned. Turn; cook 2 to 3 minutes or until browned. Add broth; reduce heat to medium-low. Cover and simmer 20 minutes or until cooked through.

3. Transfer chicken to cutting board; let stand 5 minutes. Add pasta sauce to same skillet; cook 2 to 3 minutes or until heated through, stirring occasionally. Remove and discard toothpicks from chicken. Serve chicken with squash. Top with sauce. *Makes 4 servings*

Note: To cook spaghetti squash, cut 2½-pound squash in half lengthwise; remove and discard seeds. Place, cut side down, in microwavable baking dish. Add ½ cup water. Cover; cook on HIGH 10 to 15 minutes or until soft. Let cool 15 minutes. Scrape out squash with fork. Makes about 4 cups cooked squash.

-MENU-

Stuffed Pizza

Cheesy Turkey and Vegetable Pizza

Sicilian-Style Pizza

Classic Potato, Onion & Ham Pizza

Herbed Mushroom Pizza

Italian Sausage and Bell Pepper Pizza

Plum Tomato Basil Pizza

White Pizza with Clams and Bacon

Caramelized Onion and Olive Pizza

Homemade Pizza Margherita

Super Cheese Pizza

Rustic Sausage Ricotta Pizza

Caprese Pizza

Sausage, Peppers & Onion Pizza

Classic Pepperoni Pizza

Mushroom & Goat Cheese Pizza

Stuffed Crust Pizza

Supreme Pizza

Super Slices & Perfect Pies

Stuffed Pizza

2 loaves (1 pound each) frozen bread dough, thawed

1 bottle (15 ounces) CONTADINA® Pizza Squeeze Pizza Sauce, divided

1 package (3 ounces) sliced pepperoni, quartered

1 package (10 ounces) frozen chopped spinach, thawed and squeezed dry

1 cup (4 ounces) shredded mozzarella cheese

1 carton (8 ounces) ricotta cheese

1 cup grated Parmesan cheese

1 can (3.8 ounces) sliced ripe olives, drained

1 tablespoon olive oil

1 tablespoon grated Parmesan cheese

1. Roll bread dough into two 12-inch circles on floured surface. Place one circle on greased baking sheet.

2. Spread with ¼ cup pizza sauce to 1 inch from edge.

3. Combine pepperoni, spinach, mozzarella, ricotta, 1 cup Parmesan cheese and olives in large bowl. Spread mixture over pizza sauce. Squeeze ¼ cup pizza sauce evenly over filling; dampen outside edge. Place remaining bread dough on top and seal. Cut 8 steam vents.

4. Bake on lowest rack in preheated 350°F oven for 20 minutes. Brush with olive oil; sprinkle with 1 tablespoon Parmesan cheese.

5. Bake for additional 15 to 20 minutes or until well browned. Let stand 15 minutes before cutting. Warm remaining pizza sauce and serve over wedges of pizza. *Makes 8 servings*

Prep Time: 20 minutes
Cook Time: 40 minutes

Cheesy Turkey and Vegetable Pizza

1 package (13.8 ounces) refrigerated pizza dough
4 tablespoons olive oil, divided
1 jar (14 ounces) pizza sauce
¾ pound turkey breast tenderloin, cut into 1-inch cubes
1 clove garlic, minced
1 teaspoon dried basil
1 onion, cut into thin rings
1 green bell pepper, cut into thin rings
8 ounces button mushrooms, sliced
1 can (2¼ ounces) sliced pitted black olives, drained
1 cup (4 ounces) shredded Monterey Jack cheese
1 cup (4 ounces) shredded Muenster cheese
⅓ cup grated Parmesan cheese

1. Preheat oven to 425°F. Unroll dough and press into greased 13×9-inch baking pan or 12-inch pizza pan. Brush dough with 1 tablespoon oil; spread with pizza sauce.

2. Heat remaining 3 tablespoons oil in large skillet over medium-high heat. Add turkey, garlic and basil; cook and stir 2 minutes. Add onion, bell pepper and mushrooms; cook and stir 5 minutes or until turkey is cooked through.

3. Spread turkey mixture evenly over sauce; top with olives. Sprinkle with cheeses. Bake 20 minutes or until crust is golden brown.

Makes 4 to 6 servings

Sicilian-Style Pizza

2 loaves (1 pound each) frozen white bread dough
   Vegetable cooking spray
1¾ cups PREGO® Traditional Italian Sauce
2 cups shredded mozzarella cheese (about 8 ounces)

1. Thaw the bread dough according to the package directions. Heat the oven to 375°F. Spray a 15×10-inch jelly-roll pan with cooking spray. Place the dough loaves into the pan. Press the dough from the center out until it covers the bottom of the pan. Pinch the edges of the dough to form a rim.

2. Spread the sauce over the crust. Top with the cheese.

3. Bake for 25 minutes or until the cheese is melted and the crust is golden.   *Makes 8 servings*

Kitchen Tip: To thaw the dough more quickly, place the dough into a microwavable dish. Brush with melted butter or spray with vegetable cooking spray. Microwave on LOW for 1 to 2 minutes.

Thaw Time: 3 hours
Prep Time: 10 minutes
Bake Time: 25 minutes

Classic Potato, Onion & Ham Pizza

3 tablespoons butter or olive oil, divided

3 cups new potatoes, cut into ¼-inch slices

2 sweet onions, cut into ¼-inch slices

1 tablespoon coarsely chopped garlic

½ teaspoon salt

½ teaspoon black pepper

2 cups (8 ounces) shredded Wisconsin Mozzarella cheese

1 (16-ounce) Italian-style bread shell pizza crust

8 thin slices (4 ounces) deli ham

8 slices (4 ounces) Wisconsin Provolone cheese

⅓ cup grated Wisconsin Parmesan cheese

¼ cup chopped Italian parsley

Melt 2 tablespoons butter or olive oil in large skillet over medium heat; add potatoes, onions, garlic, salt and pepper. Cook 12 to 15 minutes, turning occasionally. Add remaining 1 tablespoon butter. Cook 5 to 7 minutes or until potatoes are golden brown. Cool slightly.

Preheat oven to 400°F. Sprinkle mozzarella cheese over crust; top with ham slices. Arrange potato mixture over ham; top with provolone cheese. Sprinkle with Parmesan cheese and parsley. Place crust directly on oven rack; bake for 15 to 20 minutes or until cheese is melted.

Makes 4 servings

Favorite recipe from **Wisconsin Milk Marketing Board**

Herbed Mushroom Pizza

   2 tablespoons olive oil

   8 ounces sliced button, portobello or shiitake mushrooms

1½ teaspoons minced garlic

  ½ teaspoon dried basil

  ½ teaspoon dried thyme

  ¼ teaspoon salt

  ¼ teaspoon black pepper

  ⅓ cup pizza or marinara sauce

   1 (12-inch) prepared pizza crust

1½ cups (6 ounces) shredded mozzarella cheese

1. Preheat oven to 450°F. Heat oil in large skillet over medium-high heat. Add mushrooms and garlic; cook 4 minutes, stirring occasionally. Stir in basil, thyme, salt and pepper.

2. Spread pizza sauce evenly over crust. Top with mushroom mixture; sprinkle with mozzarella cheese. Bake directly on oven rack 8 minutes or until crust is golden brown and cheese is melted. Slide baking sheet under pizza to remove from oven. *Makes 4 servings*

Prep and Cook Time: 15 minutes

Italian Sausage and Bell Pepper Pizza

1 cup (½ of 15-ounce can) CONTADINA® Original Pizza Sauce

1 (12-inch) prepared pre-baked pizza crust

1 cup (4 ounces) shredded mozzarella cheese

½ cup (2 ounces) shredded Parmesan cheese

4 ounces (about 2 links) mild Italian sausage, cooked and sliced or crumbled

1 small green bell pepper, cut into thin strips

1. Spread pizza sauce onto crust to within 1 inch of edge.

2. Sprinkle with ½ cup mozzarella cheese, Parmesan cheese, sausage, bell pepper and remaining mozzarella cheese.

3. Bake according to pizza crust package directions or until crust is crisp and cheese is melted.   *Makes 8 servings*

Tip

Italian sausage is usually ground pork with the addition of flavorings such as garlic and fennel seed or anise seed. It comes in mild, sweet and hot varieties. You may substitute Italian turkey sausage for less fat.

Plum Tomato Basil Pizza

  1 cup (4 ounces) shredded mozzarella cheese
  1 (10-ounce) package prepared pizza crust
  4 ripe seeded Italian plum tomatoes, sliced
  ½ cup fresh basil leaves
1½ teaspoons Original TABASCO® brand Pepper Sauce
   Olive oil

Preheat oven to 425°F. Sprinkle shredded mozzarella cheese evenly over pizza crust. Layer with tomatoes and basil. Drizzle with TABASCO® Sauce and olive oil. Bake on pizza pan or stone 15 minutes or until cheese is melted and crust is golden brown.   *Makes 4 servings*

White Pizza with Clams and Bacon

  1 (10-ounce) can clams, drained
  1 (10-ounce) package prepared pizza crust
  3 strips bacon, cooked and crumbled
  2 tablespoons grated Romano cheese
  3 cloves garlic, peeled and minced
  1 teaspoon dried oregano leaves
1½ teaspoons Original TABASCO® brand Pepper Sauce
   Olive oil

Preheat oven to 450°F. Arrange clams evenly over pizza crust; top with bacon, Romano cheese, garlic and oregano. Drizzle with TABASCO® Sauce and olive oil. Bake on pizza pan or stone 15 minutes or until cheese is melted and crust is golden brown.   *Makes 4 servings*

Plum Tomato Basil Pizza

Caramelized Onion and Olive Pizza

   2 tablespoons olive oil
1½ pounds onions, thinly sliced
   2 teaspoons fresh rosemary leaves *or* 1 teaspoon dried rosemary
  ¼ cup water
   1 tablespoon balsamic vinegar
   1 cup California ripe olives, sliced
   1 (12-inch) prebaked pizza crust
   2 cups (8 ounces) shredded mozzarella cheese

Heat oil in medium nonstick skillet. Add onions and rosemary. Cook, stirring frequently, until onions begin to brown and browned bits begin to stick to bottom of skillet, about 15 minutes. Stir in ¼ cup water; scrape up any browned bits. Reduce heat to medium-low and continue to cook, stirring occasionally, until onions are golden and sweet-tasting, 15 to 30 minutes; add more water, 1 tablespoon at a time, if onion mixture appears dry. Remove pan from heat and stir in vinegar, scraping up any browned bits from pan. Gently stir in olives. Place crust on pizza pan or baking sheet. Spoon onion mixture into center of crust. Sprinkle with cheese. Bake in 450°F oven until cheese is melted and just beginning to brown, about 15 minutes. Cut into wedges and serve warm.

Makes 8 to 10 servings

Prep Time: 15 minutes
Cook Time: about 1 hour

Favorite recipe from *California Olive Industry*

Homemade Pizza Margherita

2 cups all-purpose flour

1 cup whole wheat flour

2 teaspoons salt

1 package rapid-rise active dry yeast

1 cup hot (120°F) water

3 tablespoons olive oil, divided

1 onion, chopped

2 cloves garlic, minced

1 can (about 14 ounces) fire-roasted diced tomatoes

⅓ cup red wine (optional)

½ teaspoon Italian seasoning

   Sliced plum tomatoes

   Fresh mozzarella cheese, thinly sliced

   Fresh basil leaves, torn into pieces

1. Combine all-purpose flour, whole wheat flour, salt and yeast in food processor. Process using on/off pulsing action just until combined. With machine running, add water and 2 tablespoons oil through feed tube. Process 30 seconds or until dough forms a ball. Dough should be slightly sticky. If ball does not form and dough seems too wet, add additional all-purpose flour, 1 tablespoon at a time. If too dry, add water, 1 tablespoon at a time.

2. Place dough on floured surface and knead 1 minute. Transfer dough to oiled bowl. Cover; allow to rise in warm place 45 minutes or until almost doubled.*

3. For sauce, heat remaining 1 tablespoon oil in medium saucepan over medium heat. Add onion and garlic; cook and stir 2 minutes or until softened. Add diced tomatoes, wine, if desired, and seasoning. Increase heat to medium-high; cook 5 to 10 minutes or until slightly reduced, stirring occasionally. Remove from heat; let cool. Transfer to food processor; process using on/off pulsing action until almost smooth. Refrigerate until ready to use.

4. Preheat oven to 450°F. Punch dough down and place on floured surface. Divide in half. Roll out each piece using floured rolling pin into 10- or 12-inch circle.

5. Transfer dough circles to baking sheets or pizza pans.** Spread with thin layer of sauce. (Freeze leftover sauce for later use.) Top with plum tomatoes, mozzarella and basil. Bake 6 to 10 minutes or until crust begins to brown around edges and toppings are bubbly. Top with additional basil before serving.   *Makes 6 to 8 servings*

*Dough may also be refrigerated for up to 24 hours for a slower rise. Bring dough to room temperature and proceed with recipe. Or wrap and freeze for up to 3 months.
**Sprinkle baking sheets with cornmeal before transferring dough to prevent sticking.

Super Cheese Pizza

   1 cup (½ of 15-ounce can) CONTADINA® Four Cheese Pizza Sauce
   1 (12-inch) prepared pre-baked pizza crust
   1 cup (4 ounces) cubed mozzarella cheese
   1 cup (4 ounces) cubed provolone cheese
½ cup chopped red onion
   6 to 8 ounces cooked ham, salami or turkey, cut into cubes
   2 tablespoons chopped green onion

1. Spread pizza sauce onto crust to within 1 inch of edge.

2. Top with mozzarella cheese, provolone cheese, red onion and ham.

3. Bake according to pizza crust package directions or until crust is crisp and cheese is melted. Sprinkle with green onion.   *Makes 8 servings*

Rustic Sausage Ricotta Pizza

1 cup whole milk ricotta cheese
½ cup chopped fresh basil
⅓ cup grated Parmesan cheese
2 cloves garlic, minced
½ teaspoon *each* salt and red pepper flakes
4 ounces kielbasa or other smoked sausage
1 green bell pepper, cut in half lengthwise
3 tablespoons olive or vegetable oil, divided
1 package (13.8 ounces) refrigerated pizza dough
8 slices (6 ounces) smoked provolone cheese
1 tomato, cut into 8 very thin slices

1. Prepare grill for direct cooking over medium-high heat. Combine ricotta cheese, basil, Parmesan cheese, garlic, salt and red pepper flakes in medium bowl. Stir well; set aside.

2. Grill sausage 5 minutes, turning frequently. Place bell pepper halves on grid; brush with 1 tablespoon oil. Grill 8 to 10 minutes or until sausage is brown and bell pepper is tender. Transfer to cutting board. Cut sausage and bell pepper into thin slices; set aside.

3. Brush back of baking sheet with 1 tablespoon oil. Divide dough into 4 pieces. Form each piece into ¼-inch-thick round. Place dough rounds on prepared baking sheet; brush with remaining 1 tablespoon oil. Place baking sheet directly on grid. Cook 2 minutes or until brown on the bottom. Flip and cook 1 minute or until firm but still pale in color. Remove from grill.

4. Spread rounds evenly with ricotta mixture to within 1 inch of edge. Top with provolone cheese, tomato, sausage and bell pepper.

5. Place baking sheet with pizzas on grid. Cover; cook 3 to 5 minutes or until cheese melts. Serve immediately.   *Makes 4 servings*

Caprese Pizza

1 loaf (1 pound) frozen pizza or bread dough, thawed

1 container (12 ounces) bruschetta sauce

1 container (8 ounces) pearl-size fresh mozzarella cheese (perlini),
    drained*

*If pearl-size mozzarella is not available, use 1 (8-ounce) ball of fresh mozzarella and
chop into ¼-inch pieces.*

1. Preheat oven to 400°F. Spray jelly-roll pan or baking sheet with
nonstick cooking spray.

2. Roll out dough on lightly floured surface into 15×10-inch rectangle.
Transfer to prepared pan. Cover loosely with plastic wrap; let rest
10 minutes. Meanwhile, place bruschetta sauce in colander; let drain
10 minutes.

3. Prick surface of dough several times with fork. Bake 10 minutes.
Remove from oven. Sprinkle with drained bruschetta sauce and top with
mozzarella. Bake 10 minutes or until cheese is melted and crust is golden
brown.   *Makes 6 servings*

Tip

Bruschetta sauce is a mixture of diced fresh
tomatoes, garlic, basil and olive oil. It is typically
found in the refrigerated section of the supermarket
with other prepared dips such as hummus.

Sausage, Peppers & Onion Pizza

½ pound bulk Italian sausage
1 medium red bell pepper, cut into strips
1 pre-baked pizza crust (14 inches)
1 cup spaghetti or pizza sauce
1½ cups shredded mozzarella cheese
1⅓ cups *French's*® French Fried Onions

1. Preheat oven to 450°F. Cook sausage in nonstick skillet over medium heat until browned, stirring frequently; drain. Add bell pepper and cook until crisp-tender, stirring occasionally.

2. Top pizza crust with sauce, sausage mixture and cheese. Bake 8 to 10 minutes or until cheese melts. Sprinkle with French Fried Onions; bake 2 minutes or until onions are golden. *Makes 8 servings*

Classic Pepperoni Pizza

1 cup (½ of 15-ounce can) CONTADINA® Original Pizza Sauce
1 (12-inch) prepared pre-baked pizza crust
1½ cups (6 ounces) shredded mozzarella cheese
1½ ounces sliced pepperoni
1 tablespoon chopped fresh parsley

1. Spread pizza sauce onto crust to within 1 inch of edge.

2. Sprinkle with 1 cup cheese, pepperoni and remaining cheese.

3. Bake according to pizza crust package directions or until crust is crisp and cheese is melted. Sprinkle with parsley. *Makes 8 servings*

Mushroom & Goat Cheese Pizza

1 package (13.8 ounces) refrigerated pizza dough

2 tablespoons olive oil

1 red onion, thinly sliced

3 cloves garlic, minced

1 package (8 ounces) sliced button mushrooms

1 package (6 ounces) sliced cremini mushrooms

1 package (5 ounces) sliced shiitake mushrooms

Salt and black pepper

1 package (4 ounces) goat cheese, softened

2 cups (8 ounces) shredded mozzarella cheese or pizza cheese blend, divided

¾ cup sun-dried tomatoes (not packed in oil), finely chopped

1. Preheat oven to 400°F. Spray baking sheet with nonstick cooking spray. Shape dough into large rectangle on prepared baking sheet. Bake 7 minutes or until set. Cool slightly.

2. Meanwhile, heat oil in 12-inch skillet over medium-high heat. Add onion; cook and stir 2 minutes. Add garlic; cook and stir 30 seconds. Add button and cremini mushrooms. Cook 5 minutes, stirring occasionally. Add shiitake mushrooms; season with salt and pepper. Cook 10 minutes or until liquid has evaporated.

3. Spread goat cheese on pizza crust. Sprinkle with 1½ cups mozzarella cheese and tomatoes. Top with mushroom mixture. Sprinkle with remaining ½ cup mozzarella cheese.

4. Bake 10 to 12 minutes or until cheese is melted and crust is golden brown. Serve immediately. *Makes 4 to 6 servings*

Stuffed Crust Pizza

  1 package (13.8 ounces) refrigerated pizza crust dough
  7 mozzarella cheese sticks
  ¾ cup RAGÚ® Old World Style® Pasta Sauce
  1 small red bell pepper, diced
  1 cup shredded mozzarella cheese (about 4 ounces)
12 slices pepperoni

1. On greased baking sheet, roll pizza dough into 13×10-inch rectangle. Arrange 2 cheese sticks on long edge, then 1½ cheese sticks on shorter edge. Lift pizza dough over cheese sticks and press to seal tightly. Freeze 20 minutes.

2. Meanwhile, preheat oven to 425°F. Bake pizza dough 6 minutes. Evenly top with Pasta Sauce, red pepper, shredded cheese and pepperoni.

3. Bake 6 minutes or until cheese is melted and crust is golden.

Makes 6 servings

Prep Time: 10 minutes
Chill Time: 20 minutes
Cook Time: 15 minutes

Supreme Pizza

½ cup tomato sauce

1 clove garlic, minced

½ teaspoon dried basil

½ teaspoon dried oregano

⅛ teaspoon red pepper flakes (optional)

2 grilled sausage links

1 grilled red onion

1 grilled bell pepper

1 (12-inch) prepared pizza crust

1½ cups (6 ounces) shredded fontina cheese or pizza cheese blend

½ cup grated Parmesan cheese

1. Preheat oven to 450°F. Combine tomato sauce, garlic, basil, oregano and red pepper flakes, if desired, in small bowl. Cut sausages in half lengthwise, then cut crosswise into ½-inch slices. Cut onion and bell pepper into 1-inch pieces.

2. Place pizza crust on pizza pan or baking sheet. Spread tomato sauce mixture over crust to within 1 inch of edge. Sprinkle fontina cheese over tomato sauce; top with sausage, onion and bell pepper. Sprinkle with Parmesan cheese.

3. Bake 12 minutes or until crust is crisp and cheese is melted.

Makes 4 servings

MENU

Chicken Tetrazzini with Roasted Red Peppers

Skillet Pasta Roma

Baked Ravioli with Pumpkin Sauce

Angel Hair Pasta with Seafood Sauce

Pesto Chicken Mac & Cheese

Whole Wheat Spaghetti with
Roasted Pepper Tomato Sauce

Pasta with Spinach and Ricotta

Spicy Italian Sausage & Penne Pasta

Linguine with Herbs, Tomatoes and Capers

Primavera Sauce with Artichokes and Shrimp

Chicken and Mushroom Fettuccine Alfredo

Shells and Gorgonzola

Fusilli with Broccoli Rabe

Tuscan Kalamata Olive and White Bean Pasta

Ravioli Panzanella Salad

Italian Beef Ragu

Baked Rigatoni

The Pasta Bowl

Chicken Tetrazzini with Roasted Red Peppers

6 ounces uncooked egg noodles

3 tablespoons butter

¼ cup all-purpose flour

1 can (about 14 ounces) chicken broth

1 cup whipping cream

2 tablespoons dry sherry

2 cans (6 ounces each) sliced mushrooms, drained

1 jar (about 7 ounces) roasted red peppers, drained and cut into ½-inch strips

2 cups chopped cooked chicken

1 teaspoon Italian seasoning

½ cup grated Parmesan cheese

1. Cook egg noodles according to package directions. Drain well; cover and keep warm.

2. Melt butter in medium saucepan over medium heat. Add flour; whisk until smooth. Gradually whisk in broth. Increase heat to high; bring to a boil. Remove from heat. Stir in cream and sherry until well blended.

3. Combine mushrooms, roasted peppers and noodles in large bowl; toss well. Add half of sauce to bowl; stir. Combine remaining sauce, chicken and seasoning in medium bowl.

4. Spoon noodle mixture onto serving plates. Top with chicken mixture. Sprinkle with Parmesan cheese. *Makes 6 servings*

Prep and Cook Time: 20 minutes

Skillet Pasta Roma

½ pound Italian sausage, sliced or crumbled

1 large onion, coarsely chopped

1 large clove garlic, minced

2 cans (14½ ounces each) DEL MONTE® Diced Tomatoes with Basil, Garlic & Oregano

1 can (8 ounces) DEL MONTE Tomato Sauce

1 cup water

8 ounces uncooked rotini or other spiral pasta

8 mushrooms, sliced (optional)

Grated Parmesan cheese and fresh parsley sprigs (optional)

1. Brown sausage in large skillet. Add onion and garlic. Cook until onion is soft; drain. Stir in undrained tomatoes, tomato sauce, water and pasta.

2. Cover and bring to a boil; reduce heat. Simmer, covered, 25 to 30 minutes or until pasta is tender, stirring occasionally.

3. Stir in mushrooms, if desired; simmer 5 minutes. Serve in skillet garnished with cheese and parsley, if desired.   *Makes 4 servings*

Baked Ravioli with Pumpkin Sauce

1 package (9 ounces) refrigerated cheese ravioli
1 tablespoon butter
1 shallot, finely chopped
1 cup whipping cream
1 cup solid-pack pumpkin
½ cup shredded Asiago cheese, divided
½ teaspoon salt
¼ teaspoon ground nutmeg
⅛ teaspoon black pepper
½ cup coarse plain dry bread crumbs or small croutons

1. Preheat oven to 350°F. Grease 2-quart baking dish.

2. Cook ravioli according to package directions. Drain well; cover and keep warm.

3. Melt butter in medium saucepan over medium heat. Add shallot; cook and stir 3 minutes or until tender. Reduce heat to low. Add cream, pumpkin, ¼ cup Asiago cheese, salt, nutmeg and pepper; cook and stir 2 minutes or until cheese melts. Gently stir in ravioli.

4. Transfer ravioli and sauce to prepared baking dish. Combine remaining ¼ cup Asiago cheese and bread crumbs in small bowl; sprinkle over ravioli.

5. Bake 15 minutes or until heated through and topping is lightly browned.

Makes 4 servings

Angel Hair Pasta with Seafood Sauce

½ pound firm whitefish, such as sea bass, monkfish or grouper
2 teaspoons olive oil
½ cup chopped onion
2 cloves garlic, minced
3 pounds plum tomatoes, seeded and chopped
¼ cup chopped fresh basil
2 tablespoons chopped fresh oregano
1 teaspoon red pepper flakes
½ teaspoon sugar
2 bay leaves
½ pound bay scallops or shucked oysters
8 ounces uncooked angel hair pasta
2 tablespoons chopped fresh Italian parsley

1. Cut whitefish into ¾-inch pieces; set aside.

2. Heat oil in large nonstick skillet over medium heat. Add onion and garlic; cook and stir 3 minutes or until onion is tender. Reduce heat to low. Add tomatoes, basil, oregano, red pepper flakes, sugar and bay leaves; cook 15 minutes, stirring occasionally.

3. Add whitefish and scallops; cook 3 to 4 minutes or until fish begins to flake when tested with fork and scallops are opaque. Remove and discard bay leaves.

4. Meanwhile, cook pasta according to package directions. Drain well; return to saucepan. Add sauce; toss to coat. Sprinkle with parsley. Serve immediately.   *Makes 6 servings*

Pesto Chicken Mac & Cheese

4 cups milk

1 clove garlic, peeled and smashed

¼ cup (½ stick) butter

5 tablespoons all-purpose flour

8 ounces fontina cheese, shredded

2 cups (8 ounces) shredded mozzarella cheese

½ cup grated Parmesan cheese

½ cup pesto

Salt and black pepper

1 package (6 ounces) baby spinach

1 package (16 ounces) radiatore or penne pasta, cooked and drained

1 pound boneless skinless chicken breasts, cooked and chopped

1. Bring milk and garlic to a boil in small saucepan. Reduce heat; keep warm. Discard garlic.

2. Melt butter in large saucepan over medium heat; whisk in flour. Cook and stir 2 minutes. Gradually add milk, whisking constantly until smooth. Bring to a boil. Reduce heat; cook and stir 10 minutes or until thickened. Remove from heat.

3. Add cheeses to sauce, whisking until smooth. Stir in pesto; season with salt and pepper. Toss spinach, pasta and chicken with pesto mixture until spinach wilts. Serve immediately.   *Makes 6 to 8 servings*

Whole Wheat Spaghetti with Roasted Pepper Tomato Sauce

2 tablespoons olive oil
1 red onion, finely chopped
1 clove garlic, minced
   Roasted Peppers (recipe follows),* chopped
1 can (about 14 ounces) fire-roasted diced tomatoes
½ teaspoon salt
¼ teaspoon dried oregano
¼ teaspoon chipotle chile flakes** or red pepper flakes
⅛ teaspoon black pepper
 8 ounces whole wheat spaghetti, cooked and drained
½ cup grated Parmesan cheese

*Or substitute 3 jarred roasted red bell peppers.
**Chipotle chile flakes are available in the spice section of the supermarket.*

1. Heat oil in large skillet over medium-high heat. Add onion and garlic; cook and stir 3 to 5 minutes or until tender. Add Roasted Peppers; cook 2 minutes.

2. Add tomatoes, salt, oregano, chile flakes and black pepper. Reduce heat to low; simmer 10 minutes. Serve over spaghetti; sprinkle with Parmesan cheese.   *Makes 4 servings*

Roasted Peppers: Place 3 red bell peppers on a stovetop over an open flame or 4 inches from heat in a broiler. Turn frequently to blacken all sides, using long-handled tongs. Transfer to a paper bag, shut the bag and set it aside for 30 minutes to 1 hour to loosen the skin. Scrape off the blackened skin with a paring knife.

*Whole Wheat Spaghetti with
Roasted Pepper Tomato Sauce*

Pasta with Spinach and Ricotta

8 ounces uncooked tri-colored rotini pasta
  Nonstick cooking spray
1 package (10 ounces) frozen chopped spinach, thawed and
    squeezed dry
2 teaspoons minced garlic
1 cup ricotta cheese
½ cup water
3 tablespoons grated Parmesan cheese, divided
  Salt and black pepper

1. Cook pasta according to package directions. Drain well; cover and keep warm.

2. Coat large skillet with cooking spray; heat over medium-low heat. Add spinach and garlic; cook and stir 5 minutes. Stir in ricotta cheese, water and half of Parmesan cheese. Season with salt and pepper.

3. Add pasta to skillet; stir until well blended. Sprinkle with remaining Parmesan cheese.   *Makes 4 servings*

Tip: For a special touch, garnish with fresh basil leaves.

Spicy Italian Sausage & Penne Pasta

8 ounces uncooked penne pasta
1 pound bulk hot Italian sausage
1 cup chopped sweet onion
2 cloves garlic, minced
2 cans (about 14 ounces each) seasoned diced tomatoes
3 cups broccoli florets
½ cup shredded Asiago or Romano cheese

1. Cook pasta according to package directions; drain. Return to saucepan; keep warm.

2. Meanwhile, crumble sausage into large skillet. Add onion; cook and stir over medium-high heat until sausage is cooked through. Drain fat. Add garlic; cook 1 minute. Stir in tomatoes and broccoli. Cover; cook 10 minutes or until broccoli is tender.

3. Add sausage mixture to pasta; toss well. Sprinkle with Asiago cheese.

Makes 4 to 6 servings

Tip

Asiago cheese is made from cow's milk. When young, it is relatively mild in flavor, making it a perfect addition to any cheese platter. As it ages, it becomes rich and complex. Aged Asiago cheese is an excellent alternative to Parmesan cheese when shredded or grated over pasta.

Linguine with Herbs, Tomatoes and Capers

1 package (9 ounces) refrigerated linguine
2 tablespoons olive oil
2 cups chopped tomatoes
2 cloves garlic, minced
¼ cup finely chopped green onions, green parts only
3 tablespoons capers, drained
2 tablespoons finely chopped fresh basil
    Salt and black pepper
½ cup shredded Parmesan cheese

1. Cook linguine according to package directions. Drain well; cover and keep warm.

2. Heat oil in large skillet over medium-high heat. Add tomatoes and garlic; cook 3 minutes or until tomatoes begin to soften, stirring frequently. Stir in green onions, capers and basil. Season with salt and pepper.

3. Add linguine to skillet; toss with tomato mixture. Sprinkle with Parmesan cheese.   *Makes 4 servings*

Primavera Sauce with Artichokes and Shrimp

2 tablespoons olive oil

1 cup diced carrots

1 cup diced celery

1 small onion, diced

3 cloves garlic, finely chopped

1 can (28 ounces) CONTADINA® Recipe Ready Crushed Tomatoes with Italian Herbs

½ teaspoon salt

¼ teaspoon black pepper

8 ounces medium raw shrimp, peeled and deveined

1 cup sliced artichoke hearts, drained

Fresh chopped basil (optional)

1. Heat oil in large skillet over high heat. Add carrots, celery, onion and garlic. Cook for 4 to 5 minutes or until carrots are crisp-tender.

2. Add crushed tomatoes, salt and pepper. Bring to boil. Add shrimp and artichoke hearts. Cook for 2 to 3 minutes or until shrimp turn pink.

3. Reduce heat to low; simmer for 2 minutes to blend flavors. Sprinkle with basil. Serve over hot cooked pasta or rice, if desired.

Makes 6 servings

Prep Time: 12 minutes
Cook Time: 12 minutes

Chicken and Mushroom Fettuccine Alfredo

1½ pounds chicken breast tenders
2 packages (8 ounces each) cremini mushrooms, cut into thirds
½ teaspoon salt
¼ teaspoon black pepper
¼ teaspoon garlic powder
2 packages (8 ounces each) cream cheese, cut into chunks
1½ cups grated Parmesan cheese, plus additional for garnish
1½ cups whole milk
1 cup (2 sticks) butter, cut into pieces
1 package (1 pound) uncooked fettuccine
Chopped fresh Italian parsley (optional)

Slow Cooker Directions

1. Spray slow cooker with nonstick cooking spray. Arrange chicken in single layer in bottom of slow cooker. Top with mushrooms; sprinkle with salt, pepper and garlic powder.

2. Combine cream cheese, Parmesan cheese, milk and butter in medium saucepan over medium heat. Whisk constantly until smooth and heated through. Pour over mushrooms, pushing down any that float to surface. Cover; cook on LOW 4 to 5 hours or on HIGH 2 to 2½ hours.

3. Cook fettuccine according to package directions; drain. Add to slow cooker; toss to coat. Garnish with additional Parmesan cheese and parsley. *Makes 6 to 8 servings*

Prep Time: 20 minutes
Cook Time: 4 to 5 hours (LOW) or 2 to 2½ hours (HIGH)

Shells and Gorgonzola

1 pound uncooked medium shell pasta
1 jar (24 ounces) vodka sauce
1 package (4 ounces) crumbled Gorgonzola cheese

1. Cook pasta according to package directions. Drain well; cover and keep warm. Heat sauce in medium saucepan over medium heat.

2. Toss pasta with sauce until well blended. Stir in Gorgonzola cheese just before serving. *Makes 4 to 6 servings*

Variation: Add 2 cups packed torn spinach to hot drained pasta; stir sauce into pasta and spinach. Stir in cheese and sprinkle with chopped fresh rosemary just before serving.

Fusilli with Broccoli Rabe

8 ounces uncooked fusilli pasta
1 pound broccoli rabe, trimmed and cut into 1-inch pieces
⅓ cup FILIPPO BERIO® Extra Virgin Olive Oil
1 clove garlic, minced
Salt and freshly ground black pepper
Grated pecorino cheese

Cook pasta according to package directions until al dente (tender but still firm). Drain. In large saucepan, cook broccoli rabe in boiling salted water 3 minutes or until tender. Add to colander with pasta. Drain; transfer to large bowl. In small saucepan, heat olive oil over medium heat until hot. Add garlic; cook and stir 30 seconds to 1 minute or until golden. Add to pasta mixture; toss until well coated. Season to taste with salt and pepper. Top with cheese. *Makes 3 to 4 servings*

The Pasta Bowl

Tuscan Kalamata Olive and White Bean Pasta

2 tablespoons extra-virgin olive oil
1 clove garlic, minced
½ teaspoon salt
⅛ teaspoon red pepper flakes
6 ounces uncooked rotini pasta
1 can (about 15 ounces) navy beans
1 can (about 14 ounces) diced tomatoes
½ cup pitted kalamata olives
½ cup packed spinach leaves
¼ cup pine nuts, toasted*
2 tablespoons chopped fresh basil
2 ounces crumbled feta cheese with peppercorns**

*To toast pine nuts, spread in single layer in heavy skillet. Cook and stir over medium heat 1 to 2 minutes, stirring frequently, until nuts are lightly browned. Remove from skillet immediately. Cool before using.
**If feta cheese with peppercorns is unavailable, use plain feta and season pasta mixture with ¼ teaspoon black pepper.

1. Combine oil, garlic, salt and red pepper flakes in small bowl; set aside.

2. Cook pasta according to package directions. Meanwhile, drain beans and tomatoes in colander. Pour pasta and cooking water over beans and tomatoes. Drain well. Transfer to large bowl. Add garlic mixture, olives, spinach, nuts and basil. Toss gently to blend well. Top with feta cheese.

Makes 4 servings

Ravioli Panzanella Salad

1 package (9 ounces) refrigerated cheese ravioli
2 tablespoons olive oil
2 teaspoons white wine vinegar
⅛ teaspoon black pepper
1 cup halved grape tomatoes *or* 1 chopped tomato
½ cup sliced pimiento-stuffed green olives
¼ cup finely chopped celery
1 shallot, finely chopped *or* ¼ cup finely chopped red onion
¼ cup chopped fresh Italian parsley

1. Cook ravioli according to package directions; drain well. Transfer to large serving bowl; let stand 10 minutes.

2. Whisk oil, vinegar and pepper in small bowl until well blended; pour over ravioli. Add tomatoes, olives, celery and shallot; toss gently. Sprinkle with parsley.   *Makes 4 servings*

Tip

Panzanella is a classic Italian salad that pairs a tangy vinaigrette dressing with chopped vegetables and bread cubes. It is a delicious way to use up leftover bread before it goes stale. This salad replaces with the bread with ravioli for a tasty variation.

Italian Beef Ragu

2 tablespoons olive oil

1 cup chopped onion

2 cans (about 14 ounces each) fire-roasted diced tomatoes

1 teaspoon dried oregano

1 teaspoon dried basil

⅛ teaspoon red pepper flakes or black pepper

1 package (about 17 ounces) fully cooked beef pot roast*

8 ounces uncooked fettuccine

Fully cooked beef pot roast can be found in the refrigerated prepared meats section of the supermarket.

1. Heat oil in large saucepan over medium heat. Add onion; cook 5 minutes or until translucent and slightly browned, stirring occasionally. Add tomatoes, oregano, basil and red pepper flakes. Bring to a boil over high heat. Reduce heat to low; simmer 10 minutes, stirring occasionally.

2. Remove pot roast from package; add au jus to tomato mixture. Break meat into 1- to 1½-inch pieces. Add to tomato mixture; simmer 5 to 10 minutes or until heated through.

3. Meanwhile, cook fettuccine according to package directions; drain. Serve ragu over fettuccine. *Makes 4 servings*

Baked Rigatoni

1 pound dry rigatoni
4 ounces mild Italian sausage, casings removed, sliced
1 cup chopped onion
2 cloves garlic, minced
1 can (14.5 ounces) CONTADINA® Recipe Ready Diced Tomatoes, undrained
1 can (6 ounces) CONTADINA Tomato Paste
1 cup chicken broth
1 teaspoon salt
1 cup (4 ounces) shredded mozzarella cheese, divided
½ cup (2 ounces) shredded Parmesan cheese (optional)
2 tablespoons chopped fresh basil *or* 2 teaspoons dried basil leaves, crushed

1. Cook pasta according to package directions. Drain and keep warm.

2. Meanwhile, cook sausage in large skillet for 4 to 6 minutes or until no longer pink. Remove sausage from skillet, reserving any drippings in skillet.

3. Add onion and garlic to skillet; sauté for 2 minutes. Stir in undrained tomatoes, tomato paste, broth and salt.

4. Bring to a boil. Reduce heat to low; simmer, uncovered, for 10 minutes, stirring occasionally.

5. Combine pasta, tomato mixture, sausage, ½ cup mozzarella cheese, Parmesan cheese and basil in large bowl; spoon into ungreased 13×9-inch baking dish. Sprinkle with remaining mozzarella cheese.

6. Bake in preheated 375°F oven for 10 to 15 minutes or until cheese is melted.   *Makes 8 servings*

Menu

- Grilled Swordfish Sicilian Style
- Parmesan-Herb Cornish Hens
- Braciola
- Prosciutto-Wrapped Snapper
- Risotto Bolognese
- Pollo Diavolo
- Italian-Style Pot Roast
- Osso Buco
- Tomato-Braised Lamb
- Country-Style Braised Chicken
- Steak al Forno
- Tuna Steaks with Tomatoes & Olives
- Turkey Piccata
- Tuscan Pork Loin Roast with Fig Sauce
- Italian Fish Fillets
- Tuscan Beef

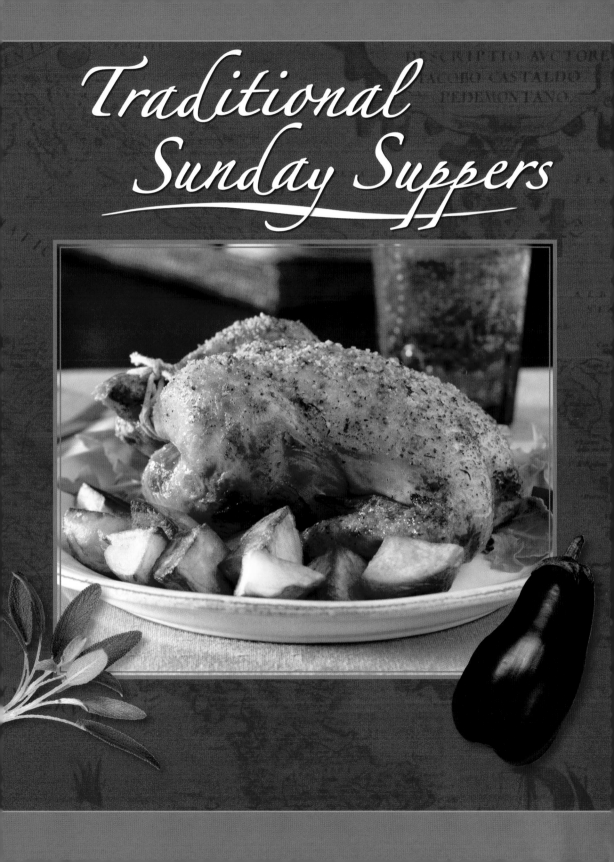

Traditional
Sunday Suppers

Grilled Swordfish Sicilian Style

3 tablespoons extra-virgin olive oil

1 clove garlic, minced

2 tablespoons lemon juice

¾ teaspoon salt

⅛ teaspoon black pepper

3 tablespoons capers, drained

1 tablespoon chopped fresh oregano or basil

1½ pounds swordfish steaks (¾ inch thick)

1. Spray grid with nonstick cooking spray. Prepare grill for direct cooking over medium heat.

2. For sauce, heat oil in small saucepan over low heat; add garlic. Cook 1 minute. Remove from heat; cool slightly. Whisk in lemon juice, salt and pepper until salt is dissolved. Stir in capers and oregano.

3. Grill swordfish 7 to 8 minutes or until fish begins to flake when tested with fork, turning once. Serve with sauce.   *Makes 4 to 6 servings*

Parmesan-Herb Cornish Hens

2 TYSON® Cornish Game Hen Twin Packs (4 total), thawed
  Salt and black pepper, to taste
¼ cup grated Parmesan cheese
2 tablespoons seasoned dry bread crumbs
1 teaspoon Italian seasoning
½ teaspoon garlic-pepper seasoning
½ teaspoon onion powder
1 teaspoon butter, melted

1. Set up grill for indirect cooking: For gas grill, preheat all burners on high. Turn one burner off; place food over "off" burner. Reset remaining burner(s) to medium. Close lid. For charcoal grill, arrange hot coals around outer edge of grill. Place disposable pan in open space; place food over open area. Close lid. Heat to medium.

2. Wash hands. Rinse hens and pat dry. Lightly salt and pepper inside of hens. Secure wings to hens and tie legs together with string, if desired. Set aside.

3. Blend Parmesan cheese, bread crumbs, seasonings and onion powder in small bowl. Rub hens with butter; sprinkle with cheese mixture, pressing lightly.

4. Place hens (not touching) over indirect heat on grill. Wash hands. Grill hens, covered, 50 to 60 minutes or until internal juices of chicken run clear. (Or insert instant-read meat thermometer into thickest part of chicken. Temperature should read 180°F.) Let stand 5 minutes before serving. Refrigerate leftovers immediately. *Makes 4 servings*

Prep Time: 25 minutes
Cook Time: 50 minutes
Total Time: 1 hour 15 minutes

Braciola

    1 can (28 ounces) tomato sauce
 2½ teaspoons dried oregano, divided
 1¼ teaspoons dried basil, divided
    1 teaspoon salt
 ½ pound bulk hot Italian sausage or sausage links, casings removed
 ½ cup chopped onion
 ¼ cup grated Parmesan cheese
    2 cloves garlic, minced
    1 tablespoon dried parsley flakes
    1 to 2 beef flank steaks (about 2½ pounds)

Slow Cooker Directions

1. Combine tomato sauce, 2 teaspoons oregano, 1 teaspoon basil and salt in medium bowl; set aside.

2. Brown sausage in large nonstick skillet over medium-high heat, stirring to break up meat. Drain fat. Combine sausage, onion, Parmesan cheese, garlic, parsley, remaining ½ teaspoon oregano and ¼ teaspoon basil in small bowl; set aside.

3. Pound steak between waxed paper to ¼-inch thickness. Cut steak into 3-inch-wide strips.

4. Spoon sausage mixture evenly onto each steak strip. Roll up, jelly-roll style, securing meat with toothpicks. Place in slow cooker. Pour tomato sauce mixture over rolls. Cover; cook on LOW 6 to 8 hours or until beef is tender.

5. Remove toothpicks; cut rolls into slices. Top with sauce.

Makes 8 servings

Prep Time: 35 minutes
Cook Time: 6 to 8 hours

Prosciutto-Wrapped Snapper

1 tablespoon plus 1 teaspoon olive oil, divided
2 cloves garlic, minced
4 skinless red snapper or halibut fillets (6 to 7 ounces each)
½ teaspoon salt
½ teaspoon black pepper
8 large fresh sage leaves
8 thin slices prosciutto (4 ounces)
¼ cup dry marsala wine

1. Preheat oven to 400°F.

2. Combine 1 tablespoon oil and garlic in small bowl; brush over fish fillets. Sprinkle with salt and pepper. Lay 2 sage leaves on each fillet. Wrap 2 slices prosciutto around fish to enclose sage leaves; tuck in ends of prosciutto.

3. Heat remaining 1 teaspoon oil in large ovenproof skillet over medium-high heat. Add fillets, sage side down; cook 3 to 4 minutes or until prosciutto is crisp. Carefully turn fish. Transfer skillet to oven; bake 8 to 10 minutes or until fish is opaque in center.

4. Transfer fish to serving plates; keep warm. Pour wine into skillet; cook over medium-high heat, stirring to scrape up browned bits. Stir constantly 2 to 3 minutes or until mixture has reduced by half. Drizzle over fish.

Makes 4 servings

Risotto Bolognese

>   1 tablespoon olive oil
>   1 medium onion, finely chopped (about ½ cup)
>   ¾ cup (6 ounces) uncooked Arborio rice (short-grain)
>   4 cups SWANSON® Chicken Broth (Regular, Natural Goodness™ or
>   Certified Organic), heated
>   1 pound ground beef
> 1½ cups PREGO® Fresh Mushroom Italian Sauce
>   ⅛ teaspoon ground black pepper
>   Shaved Parmesan cheese (optional)

1. Heat the oil in a 4-quart saucepan over medium heat. Add the onion and cook until tender. Add the rice and cook and stir for 2 minutes or until the rice is lightly browned.

2. Stir 1½ **cups** of the broth into the rice mixture. Cook and stir until the broth is absorbed, maintaining the rice at a gentle simmer. Continue cooking and adding broth ¼ **cup** at a time, stirring until it's absorbed after each addition before adding more.

3. Meanwhile, cook the beef in a 10-inch skillet over medium-high heat until it's well browned, stirring frequently to break up meat. Pour off any fat. Stir the sauce and black pepper into the skillet. Heat to a boil. Reduce the heat to low. Cook for 5 minutes or until the beef is cooked through, stirring occasionally.

4. Spoon the rice mixture on a serving platter. Spoon the beef mixture in the center. Season to taste. Serve with the cheese, if desired.

Makes 4 servings

Prep Time: 5 minutes
Cook Time: 35 minutes

Pollo Diavolo

8 skinless bone-in chicken thighs (2½ to 3 pounds)

¼ cup olive oil

3 tablespoons lemon juice

6 cloves garlic, minced

1 to 2 teaspoons red pepper flakes

3 tablespoons butter, softened

1 teaspoon dried or rubbed sage

1 teaspoon dried thyme

¾ teaspoon coarse salt

¼ teaspoon ground red pepper or black pepper

  Lemon wedges

1. Place chicken in large resealable food storage bag. Combine oil, lemon juice, garlic and red pepper flakes in small bowl. Pour mixture over chicken. Seal bag; turn to coat. Refrigerate at least 1 hour or up to 8 hours, turning once.

2. Prepare grill for direct cooking over medium-high heat. Drain chicken; reserve marinade. Place chicken on grid; brush with reserved marinade. Grill, covered, 8 minutes. Turn chicken; brush with remaining reserved marinade. Grill, covered, 8 to 10 minutes or until cooked through (165°F).

3. Meanwhile, combine butter, sage, thyme, salt and ground red pepper in small bowl; mix well. Transfer chicken to serving platter; spread herb butter over chicken. Serve with lemon wedges.

Makes 4 to 6 servings

Italian-Style Pot Roast

2 teaspoons minced garlic

1 teaspoon salt

1 teaspoon dried basil

1 teaspoon dried oregano

¼ teaspoon red pepper flakes

1 boneless beef bottom round rump or chuck shoulder roast
(2½ to 3 pounds)

1 onion, quartered and thinly sliced

1½ cups tomato-basil or marinara pasta sauce

2 cans (about 15 ounces each) cannellini or Great Northern beans,
rinsed and drained

¼ cup thinly sliced fresh basil or chopped Italian parsley

Slow Cooker Directions

1. Combine garlic, salt, dried basil, oregano and red pepper flakes in small bowl; rub over roast.

2. Place half of onion slices in slow cooker. Cut roast in half crosswise. Place half of roast over onion slices; top with remaining onion slices and other half of roast. Pour pasta sauce over roast. Cover; cook on LOW 8 to 9 hours or until roast is fork-tender.

3. Remove roast to cutting board; tent with foil. Let liquid in slow cooker stand 5 minutes. Skim off fat.

4. Turn slow cooker to HIGH. Stir beans into liquid. Cover; cook 15 to 30 minutes or until beans are heated through. Carve roast across grain into thin slices. Serve with bean mixture and fresh basil.

Makes 6 to 8 servings

Osso Buco

    3 pounds veal shanks (about 4 shanks)
       Salt and black pepper
 ½ cup all-purpose flour
    2 tablespoons olive oil
    1 cup chopped onion
    1 cup finely chopped celery
    1 cup finely chopped carrots
    2 cloves garlic, minced
 ½ cup dry white wine
    1 can (about 14 ounces) diced tomatoes
    1 cup beef broth
    1 tablespoon chopped fresh basil or rosemary leaves
    1 bay leaf
       Parmesan Gremolata (recipe follows)

1. Season veal shanks with salt and pepper. Place flour in shallow bowl; dredge veal shanks, 1 at a time, shaking off excess. Heat oil in large Dutch oven over medium-high heat. Brown veal shanks on all sides. Remove to plate.

2. Preheat oven to 350°F. Add onion, celery, carrots and garlic to Dutch oven; cook and stir 5 minutes or until soft. Add wine; cook 2 to 3 minutes, stirring to scrape up any browned bits. Add tomatoes, broth, basil and bay leaf; bring to a boil. Return veal shanks to Dutch oven; cover and bake 2 hours.

3. Meanwhile, prepare Parmesan Gremolata.

4. Remove and discard bay leaf. Serve veal shanks with vegetables. Sprinkle with Parmesan Gremolata.   *Makes 4 to 6 servings*

Parmesan Gremolata

⅓ cup grated Parmesan cheese
¼ cup chopped fresh Italian parsley
　 Grated peel of 1 lemon
1 clove garlic, minced

Combine Parmesan cheese, parsley, lemon peel and garlic in small bowl. Cover; refrigerate until ready to use.　　　　　*Makes about ⅓ cup*

Tomato-Braised Lamb

4 bone-in lamb shoulder chops (about 1 inch thick)
　 Salt and black pepper
2 onions, cut into quarters and thinly sliced
1 can (28 ounces) whole plum tomatoes, undrained
2 tablespoons *each* olive oil and red wine vinegar
3 cloves garlic, minced
1½ teaspoons dried oregano
3 to 4 sprigs fresh rosemary
　 Hot cooked polenta or pasta

1. Preheat oven to 400°F. Place lamb chops in 13×9-inch baking dish; season with salt and pepper. Top with onions.

2. Place tomatoes with juice in medium bowl; break up tomatoes. Stir in oil, vinegar, garlic and oregano. Pour mixture over lamb and onions. Tuck rosemary sprigs into tomato mixture.

3. Cover; bake 45 minutes. Turn lamb chops. Bake, uncovered, 1 hour and 15 minutes or until lamb is tender. Remove and discard rosemary sprigs. Serve with polenta or pasta.　　　　　*Makes 4 servings*

Country-Style Braised Chicken

¾ cup boiling water
½ cup dried porcini mushrooms (about ½ ounce)
¼ cup all-purpose flour
1 teaspoon salt
½ teaspoon black pepper
1 chicken, cut up (3½ to 4 pounds)
3 tablespoons olive oil
2 ounces pancetta or bacon, chopped
1 onion, chopped
2 carrots, thinly sliced
3 cloves garlic, minced
1 cup chicken broth
1 tablespoon tomato paste
1 cup pitted green Italian olives

1. Combine boiling water and mushrooms in small bowl. Let stand 15 to 20 minutes or until mushrooms are tender.

2. Meanwhile, combine flour, salt and pepper in large resealable food storage bag. Add 1 or 2 pieces of chicken at a time; toss to coat. Discard any remaining flour mixture.

3. Heat oil in large skillet over medium heat. Brown chicken on both sides. Transfer chicken to plate; set aside.

4. Pour off all but 1 tablespoon oil from skillet. Add pancetta, onion and carrots; cook 5 minutes, stirring occasionally to scrape up browned bits. Add garlic; cook 1 minute.

5. Drain mushrooms, reserving liquid. Chop mushrooms. Add mushrooms and reserved liquid to skillet. Add broth and tomato paste; bring to a boil over high heat.

continued on page 148

Country-Style Braised Chicken, continued

6. Return chicken to skillet with any juices from plate. Reduce heat; simmer 20 minutes or until chicken is cooked through (165°F) and sauce thickens, turning once. Stir in olives; cook and stir until heated through. Transfer chicken to serving platter; top with sauce.

Makes 4 to 6 servings

Steak al Forno

  4 cloves garlic, minced
  1 tablespoon olive oil
  1 tablespoon coarse salt
  1 teaspoon black pepper
  2 porterhouse or T-bone steaks (1 to 1¼ inches thick)
  ¼ cup grated Parmesan cheese

1. Prepare grill for direct cooking over medium-high heat. Combine garlic, oil, salt and pepper in small bowl; press into both sides of steaks. Let stand 15 minutes.

2. Grill steaks, covered, 7 to 10 minutes per side for medium-rare (145°F) or to desired doneness. Sprinkle Parmesan cheese over steaks during last minute of cooking.

3. Transfer to carving board; tent with foil. Let stand 5 minutes. To serve, cut meat away from each side of bone. Cut boneless pieces into slices. Serve immediately. *Makes 2 to 3 servings*

Tip: For a smoked flavor, soak 2 cups hickory or oak wood chips in cold water to cover at least 30 minutes. Drain and scatter over hot coals before grilling.

Tuna Steaks with Tomatoes & Olives

2 teaspoons olive oil
1 onion, quartered and sliced
1 clove garlic, minced
1⅓ cups chopped tomatoes
¼ cup sliced pitted black olives
2 anchovy fillets, finely chopped (optional)
2 tablespoons chopped fresh basil
¼ teaspoon salt, divided
⅛ teaspoon red pepper flakes
4 tuna steaks (¾ inch thick)
   Black pepper (optional)
   Nonstick cooking spray
¼ cup toasted pine nuts

1. Heat oil in large skillet over medium heat. Add onion; cook and stir 4 minutes. Add garlic; cook and stir 30 seconds. Add tomatoes; cook 3 minutes, stirring occasionally. Stir in olives, anchovy fillets, if desired, basil, ⅛ teaspoon salt and red pepper flakes. Cook until most of liquid is evaporated.

2. Meanwhile, sprinkle tuna with remaining ⅛ teaspoon salt and black pepper, if desired. Spray large nonstick skillet with cooking spray; heat over medium-high heat. Cook tuna 2 minutes on each side or until medium-rare. Serve with tomato mixture. Sprinkle with pine nuts.

Makes 4 servings

Turkey Piccata

2½ tablespoons all-purpose flour
¼ teaspoon salt
¼ teaspoon black pepper
1 pound turkey breast, cut into short strips
1 tablespoon butter
1 tablespoon olive oil
½ cup chicken broth
  Grated peel of 1 lemon
2 teaspoons lemon juice
2 tablespoons chopped fresh Italian parsley
2 cups cooked rice (optional)

Slow Cooker Directions

1. Combine flour, salt and pepper in resealable food storage bag. Add turkey strips and shake well to coat. Heat butter and oil in large skillet over medium-high heat. Add turkey strips; brown on all sides. Arrange in single layer in slow cooker.

2. Pour broth into skillet; cook 2 minutes, stirring to scrape up any browned bits. Pour into slow cooker. Add lemon peel and juice. Cover; cook on LOW 2 hours. Sprinkle with parsley before serving. Serve over rice, if desired.   *Makes 4 servings*

Prep Time: 15 minutes
Cook Time: 2 hours

Tuscan Pork Loin Roast with Fig Sauce

2 tablespoons olive oil

3 cloves garlic, minced

2 teaspoons coarse salt

2 teaspoons dried rosemary

½ teaspoon red pepper flakes *or* 1 teaspoon black pepper

1 center cut boneless pork loin roast (about 3 pounds)

¼ cup dry red wine

1 jar (about 8 ounces) dried fig spread

1. Preheat oven to 350°F. Combine oil, garlic, salt, rosemary and red pepper flakes in small bowl; brush over pork. Place pork on rack in shallow roasting pan.

2. Roast 1 hour or until internal temperature is 160°F. Transfer to carving board. Tent with foil; let stand 10 minutes.

3. Meanwhile, pour wine into roasting pan; cook over medium-high heat 2 minutes, stirring to scrape up any browned bits. Stir in fig spread. Cook and stir until heated through. Cut pork into thin slices; serve with sauce.   *Makes 6 to 8 servings*

Italian Fish Fillets

  2 slices **PEPPERIDGE FARM®** Sandwich White Bread, torn into
      pieces
  ⅓ cup shredded Parmesan cheese
  1 clove garlic
  ½ teaspoon dried thyme leaves, crushed
  ⅛ teaspoon ground black pepper
  2 tablespoons olive oil
  8 fresh tilapia fish fillets (3 to 4 ounces each)
  1 egg, beaten

1. Place the bread, cheese, garlic, thyme and black pepper in an electric blender container. Cover and blend until fine crumbs form. Slowly add the olive oil and blend until moistened.

2. Put the fish fillets in a 17×11-inch roasting pan. Brush with the egg. Divide the bread crumb mixture evenly over the fillets.

3. Bake at 400°F. for 10 minutes or until the fish flakes easily when tested with a fork and the crumb topping is golden.

Makes 8 servings

Easy Substitution Tip: Substitute about 2 pounds firm white fish fillets such as cod, haddock or halibut for the tilapia fillets.

Prep Time: 10 minutes
Bake Time: 10 minutes

Tuscan Beef

      1 tablespoon olive oil
      2 cloves garlic, minced
   1½ teaspoons dried rosemary, divided
      1 teaspoon salt
      ½ teaspoon black pepper
      4 beef ribeye or top loin (strip) steaks (¾ to 1 inch thick)
      ¾ cup tomato-basil or marinara pasta sauce
      ½ cup sliced pimiento-stuffed green olives
      1 tablespoon capers, drained

1. Prepare grill for direct cooking over medium high-heat or preheat broiler. Combine oil, garlic, 1 teaspoon rosemary, salt and pepper in small bowl; mix well. Spread mixture evenly over both sides of steaks.

2. Grill steaks, covered, or broil 4 inches from heat 4 to 5 minutes per side for medium-rare (145°F) or to desired doneness.

3. Meanwhile, combine pasta sauce, olives, capers and remaining ½ teaspoon rosemary in small saucepan; mix well. Cook and stir over medium heat until heated through. Serve steaks with sauce.

Makes 4 servings

Note: The sodium content of prepared pasta sauces can vary widely. Since olives and capers both add salt, choose a pasta sauce with less sodium for best results.

Menu

Cannoli Napoleons

Chilled Café Latte

Italian Soda

Nancy's Tiramisù

Blackberry Panna Cotta

Limoncello Strawberry Dessert

Smooth Mocha Coffee

Mocha Semifreddo Terrine

Chocolate Espresso Panini

Kahlúa® & Coffee

Cannoli Pastries

Orange Granita with
Balsamic and Mint Strawberries

Espresso Chocolate Cheesecake

Minted Pears with Gorgonzola

Panetonne Bread Pudding with
Caramel Sauce

Desserts & Drinks

Cannoli Napoleons

1 container (15 ounces) whole milk ricotta cheese
¾ cup mascarpone cheese
⅔ cup powdered sugar
1½ teaspoons grated orange peel
1 teaspoon vanilla
12 vanilla pizzelles
⅓ cup grated semisweet chocolate
Sweetened whipped cream
6 tablespoons chopped toasted pistachios*

To toast nuts, place in single layer on ungreased baking sheet. Bake in preheated 350°F oven 8 to 10 minutes or until lightly browned, stirring occasionally.

1. Combine ricotta cheese, mascarpone cheese, powdered sugar, orange peel and vanilla in large bowl. Cover and refrigerate 30 minutes. (Mixture can be refrigerated up to 24 hours.)

2. For each napoleon, place 1 pizzelle on dessert plate. Spread ¼ cup ricotta mixture over pizzelle. Sprinkle generous 1 teaspoon chocolate over mixture. Repeat layers. Top with dollop of whipped cream. Sprinkle with 1 tablespoon pistachios. Serve immediately.   *Makes 6 servings*

Chilled Café Latte

2 tablespoons instant coffee

¾ cup warm water

1 (14-ounce) can EAGLE BRAND® Fat Free or Original Sweetened
Condensed Milk (NOT evaporated milk)

1 teaspoon vanilla extract

4 cups ice cubes

1. In blender container, dissolve coffee in water. Add EAGLE BRAND®
and vanilla; cover and blend on high speed until smooth.

2. With blender running, gradually add ice cubes, blending until
smooth. Serve immediately. Store leftovers covered in refrigerator.

Makes about 5 cups

Prep Time: 10 minutes

Italian Soda

Ice

3 to 4 tablespoons flavored syrup

2 tablespoons half-and-half (optional)

¾ cup chilled club soda

Fill 12-ounce glass with ice. Add syrup and half-and-half, if desired. Pour
in club soda and stir. Serve immediately. *Makes 1 serving*

Nancy's Tiramisù

    6 egg yolks
1¼ cups sugar
1½ cups mascarpone cheese
1¾ cups whipping cream, beaten to soft peaks
1¾ cups cold espresso or strong brewed coffee
    3 tablespoons brandy
    3 tablespoons grappa (optional)
    4 packages (3 ounces each) ladyfingers
    2 tablespoons unsweetened cocoa powder

1. Beat egg yolks and sugar in small bowl with electric mixer at medium-high speed until pale yellow. Place in top of double boiler over simmering water. Cook, stirring constantly, 10 minutes. Combine yolk mixture and mascarpone cheese in large bowl; beat with electric mixer at low speed until well blended and fluffy. Fold in whipped cream. Set aside.

2. Combine espresso, brandy and grappa, if desired, in medium bowl. Dip 24 ladyfingers individually into espresso mixture and arrange side by side in single layer in 13×9-inch baking dish. (Dip ladyfingers into mixture quickly or they will absorb too much liquid and fall apart.)

3. Spread half of mascarpone mixture evenly over ladyfinger layer. Sift 1 tablespoon cocoa over mascarpone layer. Repeat with another layer of 24 ladyfingers dipped in espresso mixture. Cover with remaining mascarpone mixture. Sift remaining 1 tablespoon cocoa over top. Refrigerate at least 4 hours or overnight before serving.

Makes 12 servings

Substitution: If mascarpone cheese is unavailable, combine 1 package (8 ounces) softened cream cheese, ¼ cup sour cream and 2 tablespoons whipping cream in medium bowl. Beat with electric mixer at medium speed 2 minutes or until light and fluffy.

Blackberry Panna Cotta

3 cups frozen unsweetened blackberries, thawed
2 cups whipping cream
1 cup buttermilk
¾ cup sugar
3 tablespoons water
1 envelope (¼ ounce) **unflavored gelatin**

1. Process blackberries in food processor or blender until smooth. Combine cream, buttermilk and sugar in medium saucepan over medium heat. Add blackberry purée. Bring to a simmer over low heat.

2. Pour water into small saucepan. Sprinkle with gelatin; heat over low heat, swirling pan until gelatin is dissolved. Pour into blackberry mixture. Stir until combined.

3. Strain mixture through fine mesh sieve or strainer, pressing down with rubber spatula. Pour evenly into 6 (8-ounce) ramekins or custard dishes. Refrigerate 6 hours or until set. To serve, unmold onto serving plates.

Makes 6 servings

Limoncello Strawberry Dessert

1 pound strawberries
1 cup limoncello (Italian lemon liqueur), divided
1 (10-ounce) pound cake, cut into 8 slices
    Sweetened whipped cream
    Shaved chocolate
    Fresh mint leaves (optional)

1. Stem and slice strawberries. Set aside 2 cups sliced strawberries. Coarsely chop remaining strawberries; transfer to medium bowl. Stir in 2 tablespoons limoncello; let stand about 10 minutes.

2. Place 2 slices cake on each of 4 dessert plates. Drizzle 1 tablespoon limoncello over each slice.

3. Combine sliced and marinated strawberries. Evenly divide strawberry mixture over cake. Top with dollop of whipped cream. Sprinkle with chocolate. Garnish with mint leaves. Serve with remaining limoncello.

Makes 4 servings

Smooth Mocha Coffee

¾ cup hot brewed coffee
2 tablespoons HERSHEY'S Syrup
    Whipped cream (optional)
    Ground cinnamon (optional)

Stir together coffee and syrup in mug or cup. Garnish with whipped cream and cinnamon, if desired. Serve immediately.   *Makes 1 serving*

Mocha Semifreddo Terrine

1½ teaspoons espresso powder
⅓ cup boiling water
2½ cups (4 ounces) amaretti cookies (about 35 cookies)
1 tablespoon unsweetened cocoa powder
3 tablespoons butter, melted
8 egg yolks
¾ cup plus 2 tablespoons sugar, divided
1 cup whipping cream

1. Dissolve espresso powder in boiling water; set aside.

2. Line 9×5-inch loaf pan with plastic wrap. Place cookies and cocoa powder in food processor. Process until cookies are finely ground. Add butter; process until well combined. Press mixture into bottom of prepared pan. Place in freezer while preparing custard.

3. Whisk egg yolks and ¾ cup sugar in top of double boiler or medium metal bowl. Stir in cooled espresso mixture. Place over simmering water. Cook 4 to 5 minutes or until mixture thickens, whisking constantly. Remove from heat; place bowl in pan of ice water. Whisk mixture 1 minute. Let stand in ice water 5 minutes or until cooled to room temperature, whisking occasionally.

4. Beat cream and remaining 2 tablespoons sugar in large bowl with electric mixer at high speed until stiff peaks form. Gently fold whipped cream into cooled custard. Spread mixture over crust in pan. Cover tightly; freeze until firm, at least 8 hours or up to 24 hours before serving.

5. To serve, invert terrine onto serving plate; remove plastic wrap. Cut into slices. Serve on chilled plates.   *Makes 8 to 12 servings*

Chocolate Espresso Panini

2 tablespoons chocolate-hazelnut spread
¼ teaspoon instant espresso powder
2 slices rustic Italian bread
  Butter-flavored cooking spray

1. Preheat indoor grill.* Combine chocolate spread and espresso powder in small bowl; mix well. Spread chocolate mixture evenly over 1 slice bread; top with second slice.

2. Spray sandwich lightly with cooking spray. Grill 2 to 3 minutes or until bread is golden brown.   *Makes 1 panini*

*Panini can also be made on the stove in a ridged grill pan or in a nonstick skillet. Cook sandwich over medium heat about 2 minutes per side.

Kahlúa® & Coffee

1½ ounces KAHLÚA® Liqueur
  Hot coffee
  Whipped cream (optional)

Pour Kahlúa® into steaming cup of coffee. Top with whipped cream.
                                    Makes 1 serving

Cannoli Pastries

18 to 20 Cannoli Pastry Shells (page 178)
4 cups (32 ounces) ricotta cheese
1½ cups sifted powdered sugar, plus additional for garnish
2 teaspoons ground cinnamon
¼ cup diced candied orange peel, minced
1 teaspoon grated lemon peel
2 squares (1 ounce each) semisweet chocolate, finely chopped

1. Prepare Cannoli Pastry Shells; set aside.

2. For cannoli filling, beat ricotta cheese in large bowl with electric mixer at medium speed until smooth. Add powdered sugar and cinnamon; beat at high speed 3 minutes. Add candied orange peel and lemon peel; mix well. Cover and refrigerate until ready to serve.

3. To assemble, spoon cheese filling into pastry bag fitted with large plain tip. Pipe about ¼ cup filling into each Cannoli Pastry Shell.*

4. Roll Cannoli Pastries in additional powdered sugar to coat. Dip ends of pastries into chocolate. Serve immediately.

Makes 18 to 20 pastries

Do not fill Cannoli Pastry Shells ahead of time or shells will become soggy.

continued on page 178

Cannoli Pastries, continued

Cannoli Pastry Shells

1¾ cups all-purpose flour
2 tablespoons sugar
1 teaspoon grated lemon peel
2 tablespoons cold butter
6 tablespoons sweet marsala wine
1 egg
    Vegetable oil

1. Combine flour, sugar and lemon peel in medium bowl; cut in butter with 2 knives or pastry blender until mixture resembles fine crumbs. Beat marsala and egg in small bowl; add to flour mixture. Stir with fork to form ball. Divide dough in half; shape into 2 (1-inch-thick) squares. Wrap in plastic wrap and refrigerate at least 1 hour.

2. Heat 1½ inches oil in large saucepan to 325°F. Working with 1 square of dough at a time, roll out on lightly floured surface to ¹⁄₁₆-inch thickness. Cut into 9 or 10 (4×3-inch) rectangles.

3. Wrap each rectangle of dough around greased metal cannoli form or uncooked cannelloni pasta shell. Brush one edge of rectangle of dough lightly with water; overlap with opposite edge and press firmly to seal.

4. Fry 2 or 3 pastry shells at a time 1 to 1½ minutes or until light brown, turning once. Remove with tongs; drain on paper towels.

5. Set aside until cool enough to handle. Carefully remove pastry shells from cannoli forms or pasta shells; cool completely.

Makes 18 to 20 pastry shells

Orange Granita with Balsamic and Mint Strawberries

¼ **cup sugar**

1¾ **cups Florida orange juice, divided**

¼ **teaspoon ground black pepper (optional)**

1 **tablespoon lemon juice**

3 **cups sliced fresh strawberries**

3 **tablespoons fresh mint, cut into long, thin strips**

1 **tablespoon balsamic vinegar**

1. Place sugar, ¼ cup orange juice and pepper, if desired, in small saucepan; bring mixture to a boil. Remove from heat and stir in remaining 1½ cups orange juice and lemon juice.

2. Pour mixture into 13×9-inch shallow pan and place in freezer.

3. Every few minutes, stir and scrape mixture with spoon to create an icy texture. This procedure takes about 30 to 45 minutes, depending on freezer temperature.

4. Combine strawberries, mint and balsamic vinegar in small bowl; marinate while granita freezes.

5. To serve, place 2 ounces granita in individual dessert bowls; top with 3 ounces strawberry mixture.   *Makes 6 servings*

Favorite recipe from *Florida Department of Citrus*

Espresso Chocolate Cheesecake

1 package (about 10 ounces) fudge brownie mix

¼ cup *each* vegetable oil and water

4 eggs

1 cup (6 ounces) semisweet chocolate chips

⅓ cup whipping cream

1 to 2 tablespoons instant coffee granules

3 packages (8 ounces each) cream cheese, softened

¼ cup (½ stick) unsalted butter, softened

1 cup sugar

1 teaspoon vanilla

1 jar (10 ounces) raspberry fruit spread

   Whipped cream and raspberries (optional)

1. Preheat oven to 350°F. Grease 9-inch springform pan.

2. Combine brownie mix, oil, water and 1 egg in medium bowl; mix well. Pour batter into prepared pan. Bake 20 minutes or until toothpick inserted 2 inches from edge comes out clean. Cool in pan on wire rack.

3. Heat chocolate chips, cream and coffee granules in small heavy saucepan over medium-low heat until smooth, stirring frequently. Remove from heat; let stand 10 to 15 minutes.

4. Beat cream cheese and butter in large bowl with electric mixer at medium-high speed until smooth. Add sugar; beat until light and fluffy. Add remaining 3 eggs, 1 at a time, beating well after each addition. Add vanilla and melted chocolate mixture; beat at low speed just until blended.

5. Remove lid from fruit spread. Microwave on HIGH 30 seconds; stir. (Jar may be very hot.) Pour melted spread evenly over crust. Pour cheesecake batter evenly over fruit spread.

continued on page 182

Espresso Chocolate Cheesecake, continued

6. Bake 40 minutes or until edges are set but center is still moist. Cool completely in pan on wire rack. Cover and refrigerate 24 hours. Let stand 30 minutes at room temperature before serving. Serve with whipped cream and raspberries, if desired.

Makes 1 (9-inch) cheesecake

Minted Pears with Gorgonzola

4 whole firm pears with stems, peeled
2 cups Concord grape juice
1 tablespoon finely chopped fresh mint
1 tablespoon honey
1 cinnamon stick
¼ teaspoon ground nutmeg
¼ cup crumbled Gorgonzola cheese

1. Place pears in medium saucepan. Add grape juice, mint, honey, cinnamon stick and nutmeg; bring to a boil over high heat. Reduce heat to low; simmer, covered, 15 to 20 minutes, turning pears once to absorb juices evenly. Cook until pears can be pierced easily with fork. Remove pan from heat; cool. Remove pears with slotted spoon; set aside. Discard cinnamon stick.

2. Bring juice mixture to a boil. Reduce heat and simmer 20 minutes. Place pears on individual serving plates. Pour juice mixture over pears. Sprinkle Gorgonzola cheese evenly around pears. *Makes 4 servings*

Panetonne Bread Pudding with Caramel Sauce

½ (2-pound) loaf panetonne bread, cut into ¾-inch cubes (8 cups)

6 eggs

½ cup sugar

3 cups half-and-half

1 teaspoon vanilla

½ teaspoon ground cinnamon

¼ teaspoon salt

    Caramel ice cream topping

1. Preheat oven to 350°F. Grease 11×7-inch baking dish.

2. Arrange bread cubes in dish. Combine eggs and sugar in large bowl; whisk in half-and-half, vanilla, cinnamon and salt. Pour mixture over bread, pressing down to moisten top. Let stand 15 minutes.

3. Bake 40 to 45 minutes or until puffed and golden brown. Serve warm or at room temperature. Drizzle with caramel topping.

Makes 12 servings

Serving Suggestion: Dust bread pudding lightly with powdered sugar and serve caramel topping on the side.

Acknowledgments

The publisher would like to thank the companies and organizations listed below for the use of their recipes and photographs in this publication.

California Olive Industry

Campbell Soup Company

Del Monte Foods

EAGLE BRAND®

Filippo Berio® Olive Oil

Florida Department of Citrus

The Hershey Company

The Kahlúa® Liqueur trademark is used under permission from The Kahlúa Company, Purchase NY

McIlhenny Company (TABASCO® brand Pepper Sauce)

Reckitt Benckiser Inc.

Recipes courtesy of the Reynolds Kitchens

Tyson Foods, Inc.

Unilever

Wisconsin Milk Marketing Board

Index

Index

Index

Metric Conversion Chart

VOLUME MEASUREMENTS (dry)

$1/8$ teaspoon = 0.5 mL
$1/4$ teaspoon = 1 mL
$1/2$ teaspoon = 2 mL
$3/4$ teaspoon = 4 mL
1 teaspoon = 5 mL
1 tablespoon = 15 mL
2 tablespoons = 30 mL
$1/4$ cup = 60 mL
$1/3$ cup = 75 mL
$1/2$ cup = 125 mL
$2/3$ cup = 150 mL
$3/4$ cup = 175 mL
1 cup = 250 mL
2 cups = 1 pint = 500 mL
3 cups = 750 mL
4 cups = 1 quart = 1 L

VOLUME MEASUREMENTS (fluid)

1 fluid ounce (2 tablespoons) = 30 mL
4 fluid ounces ($1/2$ cup) = 125 mL
8 fluid ounces (1 cup) = 250 mL
12 fluid ounces ($1 1/2$ cups) = 375 mL
16 fluid ounces (2 cups) = 500 mL

WEIGHTS (mass)

$1/2$ ounce = 15 g
1 ounce = 30 g
3 ounces = 90 g
4 ounces = 120 g
8 ounces = 225 g
10 ounces = 285 g
12 ounces = 360 g
16 ounces = 1 pound = 450 g

DIMENSIONS

$1/16$ inch = 2 mm
$1/8$ inch = 3 mm
$1/4$ inch = 6 mm
$1/2$ inch = 1.5 cm
$3/4$ inch = 2 cm
1 inch = 2.5 cm

OVEN TEMPERATURES

250°F = 120°C
275°F = 140°C
300°F = 150°C
325°F = 160°C
350°F = 180°C
375°F = 190°C
400°F = 200°C
425°F = 220°C
450°F = 230°C

BAKING PAN SIZES

Utensil	Size in Inches/Quarts	Metric Volume	Size in Centimeters
Baking or Cake Pan (square or rectangular)	8×8×2	2 L	20×20×5
	9×9×2	2.5 L	23×23×5
	12×8×2	3 L	30×20×5
	13×9×2	3.5 L	33×23×5
Loaf Pan	8×4×3	1.5 L	20×10×7
	9×5×3	2 L	23×13×7
Round Layer Cake Pan	8×1½	1.2 L	20×4
	9×1½	1.5 L	23×4
Pie Plate	8×1¼	750 mL	20×3
	9×1¼	1 L	23×3
Baking Dish or Casserole	1 quart	1 L	—
	1½ quart	1.5 L	—
	2 quart	2 L	—